Jack London's
The Sea Wolf

Jack London's
The Sea Wolf
A Screenplay

By Robert Rossen

Edited by Rocco Fumento and
Tony Williams

Southern
Illinois University
Press
CARBONDALE AND
EDWARDSVILLE

Copyright © 1941 Turner Entertainment Co.
All rights reserved
Published by Arrangement with
Turner Entertainment Co.

"The Reality of the Nightmare"
by Rocco Fumento and
"From Novel to Film"
by Tony Williams
Copyright © 1998 by the Board of Trustees
Southern Illinois University
All rights reserved
Printed in the
United States
of America
01   00   99   98   4   3   2   1

Library of Congress Cataloging-in-Publication Data
Rossen, Robert, 1908–1966.
Jack London's The sea wolf : a screenplay / Robert Rossen ; edited
by Rocco Fumento and Tony Williams.
p.   cm.
Includes bibliographical references.
1. Sea wolf (Motion picture)   2. London, Jack, 1876–1916. Sea-wolf.   3. London, Jack, 1876–1916 Sea-wolf—Film and video adaptations.   I. Fumento, Rocco, 1923–   .   II. Williams, Tony, 1946 Jan. 11.   III. Title.
PN1997.S3195R67   1998
791.43'72—DC21   97-26704   CIP
ISBN 0-8093-2179-3 (cloth : alk. paper). — ISBN 0-8093-2176-9
(pbk. : alk. paper)

The paper used in this publication meets the minimum requirements of American National Standard for Information Sciences—Permanence of Paper for Printed Library Materials, ANSI Z39.48-1984. ♾

Contents

Acknowledgments
vii

The Reality of the Nightmare
Rocco Fumento
ix

From Novel to Film
Tony Williams
xvii

Cast of Characters
1

Jack London's *The Sea Wolf*:
A Screenplay
3

Notes
185

Acknowledgments

We wish to acknowledge
the legal department
of Turner Network Television
for their kind generosity in
allowing us access to the
Warner Brothers screenplay
of *The Sea Wolf*.

The Reality of the Nightmare
Rocco Fumento

Whether by accident or design, *The Sea Wolf*[1] is not what it first appears to be, what the critics said it was, or what Warner Brothers advertised it as being.

The advance publicity on *The Sea Wolf* stresses that it is a film of "fast, continuous action" and that "Michael Curtiz, supreme master of the outdoor film, has directed *The Sea Wolf* with rare dramatic force." Another story from the Warners press book states, "As would be expected of a film directed by Michael Curtiz, *The Sea Wolf* is a succession of moving episodes, with physical action dominant. There are forty-seven fights in the picture. All are marked by primal brutality." "Action" is the word that appears over and over again in these press releases and over and over again we are told about those forty-seven fights.[2] Naturally, Warners had its eye on the box office since the studio's and Curtiz's most successful films included such "action" films as *Captain Blood* (1935), *The Charge of the Light Brigade* (1936), *Kid Galahad* (1937), *The Adventures of Robin Hood* (1938), *Dodge City* (1939), and *The Sea Hawk* (1940). Included in the advance publicity is a quote reputedly from Curtiz himself: "I have always said that I love action in pictures and finally I found my ideal picture: one that is all action."

Like the press releases, the ads for *The Sea Wolf* also lead us to believe that it is an excitement-and-action-oriented film. These ads depict a fight scene and invariably include the scene in which Barry Fitzgerald (Cooky) threatens Alexander Knox (Van Weyden) with a knife. The most colorful ad also includes the most colorful prose: "POWER . . . FURY . . . RAGING . . . HATE . . . FEAR . . . UNFORGETTABLE!" The quotation marks lead us to believe that the words have been lifted from a review written by a well-known critic. Instead they are lifted from the studio's own publicity blurb, a blurb in which each of the key words is capitalized: "The POWER and FURY of the RAGING sea surged from the pen of Jack London as he wrote this story of HATE-ridden 'Wolf' Larsen and his FEAR-crazed crew! And now, the year's greatest cast brings it to the screen . . . every scene alive . . . and UNFORGETTABLE!" Finally, the words "Jack London's greatest novel of terror afloat" are slashed beneath the title.

With such an advertising campaign and coming upon the heels of Curtiz's similarly titled *The Sea Hawk*, it is little wonder that the public and critics alike mistook the film as being another in the series of Warner adventure epics. Bosley Crowther did comment upon the fact that "Wolf" Larsen is presented with "scrupulous psychological respect" and that he "is exposed as just a bundle of psychoses," yet even he saw the film as being mainly an action film wherein "the slapping and cuffing are done with impressive visibility and in a manner distinctive to Warner films." Still, Crowther was aware enough to realize that the film was not the usual escapist-action Warner-Curtiz film (*Captain Blood*), but more in the tradition of their realistic-action films (*Kid Galahad*). This is why he feels that "a major fault" of the film is that it does not achieve the realism it is striving for because it was too obviously "photographed in a tank, where the water laps as in a bathtub and the fog rolls like a steamroom mist. At least a good half of the effect in a sea-picture comes from the sea, and when that element is lacking the whole thing seems flat and synthetic."[3]

Other critics saw the film mainly as an action film. *Variety* regarded *The Sea Wolf* as "a strong adventure drama that will sail a profitable course through theatre boxoffices."[4] *Time* commented, "For restless cinema addicts whom only blood and thunder can quiet, *The Sea Wolf* should prove a strong sedative."[5] *Newsweek* stated nothing really different. "The current version—if anything—is more brutal than the old silent film . . . aside from a fine cast, its principal contribution to entertainment is a scriptful of violence for excitement's sake."[6]

Like Bosley Crowther, critic Welford Beaton sees the film as being realistic. Unlike Crowther, he was impressed with the creations of the studio's special effects department: "Physically, *The Sea Wolf* is an extraordinary achievement, one which will astonish you with the vividness of the impression of realism it conveys. We see ships fade into banks of fog, we see one lashed by a furious gale and shuddering under the force of the great waves whose plaything it is. . . . The thought that the entire production was photographed on a Warners stage is almost enough in itself to keep you entertained."[7] However, the same issue saw his praise of the forgettable *Penny Serenade* and *That Hamilton Woman* and his dismissal of *Citizen Kane* with "I was more bored than entertained."

Even Tom Flinn and John Davis in their otherwise intelligent and perceptive article "Warner's War of the Wolf" mention the "realistic flavor" of various scenes as staged by Michael Curtiz, including the ramming of the *Martinez*.[8] About this scene, I can only repeat what

Bosley Crowther says above: It was too obviously "photographed in a tank."

Yet Flinn and Davis also recognize the fact that "in its central concern with the darker side of human nature and the urge toward power for its own sake, *The Sea Wolf* is thematically characteristic of that group of films today known as *films noirs*."[9] At the same time it is incomprehensible that Alain Silver and Elizabeth Ward in their *Film Noir: An Encyclopedic Reference to the American Style* should ignore the film completely even in their appendix under the heading "The Period Film," seeing the period *noir* film as "an offshoot of Victorian melodrama."[10] They cite John Brahm's *The Lodger* (1944) as a prime example. "The image is nightmarish, filled with shots of the hulking lodger wandering through the dimly-lit, fog-covered streets . . . on his perverse mission of revenge."[11] Among other examples of period *noir* films they list Edgar G. Ulmer's *Bluebeard* (1944), George Cukor's *Gaslight* (1944), Brahm's follow-up to *The Lodger*, *Hangover Square* (1945), and Robert Siodmak's *The Suspect* (1945). Most of these films, they say, had "a quasi-romantic narrative accentuated by a dark and sinister atmosphere." They add, "To a certain extent this may be traced to a European sensibility latent in the work of such directors like Siodmak, Ulmer, Brahm, and even Hitchcock."[12] It is odd that they omit Curtiz who had made films in Germany and directed a version of *The Sea Wolf* that Charles Higham describes as a "Germanic, powerful work almost devoid of compromise."[13]

Is *The Sea Wolf*, then, a "realistic action film," a "period" *noir* film, or is it "Germanic"? It is all of these and yet none of them, except superficially. What Curtiz creates in this film is the reality of a nightmare, of a world that we see in Kafka or in some of Hitchcock's best films, most notably *Vertigo* and *Psycho*. Bosley Crowther indicates his lack of perceptivity when he says, "At least a good half of the effect in a sea-picture comes from the sea, and when that element is lacking the whole thing seems flat and synthetic."[14] Despite its title, the film is not a "sea-picture"; and what Crowther deems "flat and synthetic" is what helps to make the film nightmarish. Our nightmares are very real to us—so real that we wake up trembling, in a sweat. At the same time nothing is real; everything is "flat and synthetic" . . . and claustrophobic. Even a vast, sun-drenched and apparently safe plain closes in on us, as it closes in on Cary Grant in that most famous scene from *North By Northwest*. Time shrinks or is stretched out; a sea is familiar and yet we are lost; the living are dead and the dead rise again.

The opening titles of early 1940s films were rarely imaginative. Not so the titles of *The Sea Wolf*. Like Hitchcock's wrenching-apart titles for *Psycho*, they tell the tale. We see a pinpoint of white against black, the pinpoint balloons and zooms menacingly toward us to form the titles; then the titles smash into the camera and self-destruct. In the background Erich Wolfgang Korngold's music is as discordant and shattering as Bernard Herrmann's music for *Psycho*. Just as Norman Bates's split personality is foreshadowed by the titles from *Psycho*, so is the egomania of Wolf Larsen and his ultimate destruction foreshadowed by those ballooning pinpoints of white light while Korngold's music is like chalk screeching erratically across a blackboard, making us edgy, tense, apprehensive.

The opening of *The Sea Wolf* sets the tone of the entire film with its brooding blending of shadows, darkness, and fog.[15] Using tight framing, Curtiz gives us an establishing shot of San Francisco in 1900. He reveals no panoramic view of the city, no shot of the harbor and the Golden Gate. Instead we see merely a gaslit lamppost and hear and see a horse-drawn carriage careening by. Then a figure (John Garfield as George Leach) looms out of the darkness. Leach pauses and looks furtively over his shoulder and then hurries into the 8 Bells Bar. A female singer is heard singing "Hello My Baby" and later "Rosie, You Are My Posie," but we never see her. There is no panning shot of the saloon. Again the framing is tight and the camera sticks closely to Leach as he sits in the bar.

Curtiz rarely uses loose framing. Early in the film we are introduced to Van Weyden and Ruth in the roomy, main lounge of the ferryboat. The lounge, washed in shadows, is deserted. Where are the other passengers? Are we to assume that they are all out on deck on this dark, damp, and foggy night? Like Sartre's characters in *No Exit*, Van Weyden and Ruth, alone, surrounded by doors and windows that stare into a blank nothingness, seem trapped in some private hell, or, at the very least, caught in a Kafka-like nightmare. The large room shrinks oppressively, and what begins as a loosely framed scene dissolves into a claustrophobic tightly framed scene.

During the film there are several shots of the *Ghost*, white sails above a gray sea and against a gray, sometimes black, fog-shrouded background. One would expect these scenes to give the impression of open spaces and loose framing. They do not. As Crowther says in his review, such scenes were obviously "photographed in a tank, where the water laps as in a bathtub and the fog rolls like a steam-room mist."[16] He is right, of course. Yet this fakery does not, as Crowther states, work

The Reality of the Nightmare   xiii

against the film unless one thinks, as he does, that *The Sea Wolf* is "a sea-picture." The fakery, the confines of a bathtub, so to speak, turn loose framing into tight framing with the miniature vessel squeezed between studio tank water and painted backdrops. We see no distant horizons, no faraway moon or stars or sun. The ship is most certainly not a real ship sailing into a real horizon over a real sea. It is called *Ghost* and it is indeed a ghostly vessel, the kind one encounters in nightmares, whether conjured up by our imaginations or by the ingenuities of special effects men on a Hollywood sound stage.

Flip through the pages of the screenplay. Note that most of the shots indicated by Rossen are close-ups or tight or medium shots. Even when Rossen requests a panning shot, the shot is more often than not described as a medium panning shot rather than a long one. Note the deck scenes, particularly the scene in which Louie leaps to his death from the mast. Even these medium to long shots are tightly framed so that we see little of sea and sky, little of anything but the ship and its crew.

With so much tight framing it is not surprising that the film is claustrophobic. But it is not Sol Polito's camera alone, not even in conjunction with his chiaroscuro low-key lighting, that achieves this feeling of claustrophobia. Much of the credit belongs to Curtiz. Yet one wonders how much credit belongs to whom? Curtiz and Polito had worked on a number of films together before *The Sea Wolf*, including *The Charge of the Light Brigade, The Adventures of Robin Hood, The Private Lives of Elizabeth and Essex, Virginia City* (1940), and *The Sea Hawk*. Undoubtedly, each knew what the other wanted, how a film should look, how to achieve that look, what effect they wished to create upon audiences. Oddly enough, with the possible exception of *The Private Lives of Elizabeth and Essex*, all of these earlier films were mainly loosely framed: open, airy, with the camera constantly pulling back to reveal Errol Flynn leading a cast of hundreds into combat.

By using much tighter framing in *The Sea Wolf*, one feels that Curtiz and Polito knew exactly what they were doing and what kind of film they were making. If the film had been intended as a "sea-picture," think what they would have done with the following typical "sea-picture" scenes: the ramming and sinking of the *Martinez* and the assault of the *Macedonia* upon the *Ghost*. Both of these scenes are handled intimately in rapid and hallucinatory close-ups, and neither lasts for more than a minute. Curtiz and Polito had just completed *The Sea Hawk*. They knew how to expand short, intimate scenes into lengthy spectacular ones. Why not do so on *The Sea Wolf*? Did they want to save money? Warner Brothers was known as a penny-pinching studio. But they also supplied any item needed for films they felt would make money.

Has the man forever immortalized by a line from David Niven's autobiography, *Bring on the Empty Horses*, been misjudged by cinema history? Curtiz has never been included among the great directors such as John Ford, Howard Hawks, Orson Welles, Howard Hawks, Alfred Hitchcock, and Raoul Walsh among adherents of the "auteur theory." Yet there may be more to Curtiz than meets the eye. He was obviously a talent highly alert to the creative movements of his time such as German expressionism, the genius of the Hollywood studio system, genres such as *film noir*, and the possibilities offered by talented stars. A director may also be a controlling center mobilizing various contemporary creative people and stylistic forces operating at a particular time. Perhaps Curtiz deserves credit for consciously recognizing the times he lived in and the themes he responded to, particularly with a film such as *The Sea Wolf*, which reworks Jack London's original novel to take account of the different historical circumstances of the pre–Pearl Harbor world of victorious totalitarian dictatorships. Curtiz would later become the man who directed *Casablanca* (1943), a film which would speak to a different world situation than the pessimistic one of *The Sea Wolf*. Both films have equal claims to be regarded as important political allegories, particularly the latter with its mixture of German expressionism, *film noir*, and Warner Brothers version of proletarian solidarity. Although Sidney Rosenzweig never analyzes *The Sea Wolf* in his study of the films of Michael Curtiz, he does describe it as "one of Curtiz's strongest, richest movies."[17] We know little, if anything of Curtiz's political beliefs at the time so we can only speculate about how knowledgeable he was about the allegorical nature of *The Sea Wolf*. But we do have the film as an example of a common visual signature, and from there we can move on to further debate. What better way to conclude than by quoting from one book devoted to the director?

> The most obvious aspect of Curtiz's directorial signature is his expressionistic visual style, and its most obvious feature is its unusual camera angles and carefully detailed, crowded, complex compositions, full of mirrors and reflections, smoke and fog, and physical objects, furniture, foliage, bars, and windows, that stand between the camera and the human characters and seem to surround and entrap them.[18]

The Sea Wolf contains many of the above features in its allegorical depiction of a very real nightmare for those surviving the Great Depression to continue living in the grim days of 1940 when Nietzsche's Superman, personified and bastardized by Adolph Hitler, was spreading a new pestilence upon the land. Warner Brothers, whose films more than any others in Hollywood, reflected and commented upon controversial issues ripped from the headlines, led the parade of films in their fight against Hitler with its hard-hitting, semi-documentary *Confessions of a Nazi Spy* and its metaphorical but no less hard-hitting *The Sea Wolf*.

Notes

1. The title of the novel usually has a hyphen as in the original publication. However, the film's title never contains this punctuation.
2. An example of Warner Brothers hyperbole. The film is a mere eighty-seven minutes long: this averages out to more than one fight every two minutes.
3. Bosley Crowther, *New York Times*, 22 March 1941.
4. *Variety*, 26 March 1941.
5. Quoted by James Beaver, *John Garfield, His Life and Films* (South Brunswick, NJ: A. S. Barnes, 1978), 93.
6. Beaver, *John Garfield*, 93.
7. Welford Beaton, "Comments on Current Pictures," *Hollywood Spectator*, 15.7 (1 May 1941): 10.
8. Tom Flinn and John David, "Warner's War of the Wolf," in *The Classic American Novel and the Movies*, eds. Gerald Peary and Roger Shatzkin (New York: Frederick Ungar Publishing, 1977), 195–205.
9. Flinn and David, "Warner's War of the Wolf," 204.
10. *Film Noir: An Encyclopedic Reference to the American Style*, 3d ed., eds. Alain Silver and Elizabeth Ward (Woodstock, NY: Overlook Press, 1992), 327.
11. *Film Noir*, 328.
12. *Film Noir*, 328.
13. Charles Higham, *The Art of the American Film* (New York: Anchor Books, 1974), 143.
14. Higham, *The Art of the American Film*, 143.
15. Warner Brothers had purchased new fog machines just prior to the filming of *The Sea Wolf*. Along with *Out of the Fog*, *The Sea*

Wolf became a showcase for these machines. Byron Haskin and Nathan Levinson of the Warner Brothers special effects department gained an Academy Award nomination for their work on *The Sea Wolf*. See John Culhane, *Special Effects in the Movies* (New York: Ballantine, 1981), 27.
16. Culhane, *Special Effects in the Movies*, 27.
17. Sidney Rosenzweig, *Casablanca and Other Major Films of Michael Curtiz* (Ann Arbor, MI: UMI Research Press, 1982), 159.
18. Rosenzweig, *Casablanca and Other Major Films*, 157.

From Novel to Film
Tony Williams

As many critics have recognized, Jack London's *The Sea-Wolf* is a highly complex novel. It mixes political critique of the system of capitalist exploitation still with us today with a quest for personal integration that London sought throughout his entire life. As a life-long socialist who experienced the harsh conditions of industrial exploitation, Jack London spoke out against a dehumanizing system of violence and oppression both in his political writings such as *The War of the Classes* and also within his fictional work. He began writing *The Sea-Wolf* at a time of great personal trauma. During 1903 he had separated from his wife and two daughters and fallen in love with Charmian Kittredge whom he realized more appropriately embodied the ideal of "mate-woman" he sought throughout his life and fiction. While writing *The Sea-Wolf*, he explored his own type of divided self, contrasting two modes of human experience—the dehumanized brutalization affecting those at the bottom of the social scale and the effete bourgeois mentality wherein the privileged members of a class society attempt to define their unique claim to superiority. Jack London had risen up the social ladder by his stubborn persistence in becoming a best-selling writer. He could become the weak literary figure personified by Humphrey Van Weyden. But the ghost of Wolf Larsen haunted him, a ghost embodying all the vicious aspects of life at the bottom of the social pit that London had encountered as well as the dark elements in his own personality. In writing *The Sea-Wolf*, Jack London engaged in his own literary rite of integration. He showed how his hero, Van Weyden, eventually became a balanced human being by rejecting the worst aspects of Wolf Larsen, a Frankenstein monster created by the system, as well as avoiding the debilitating traps of a civilization ready to inoculate ideologically all those from other classes who succeeded in penetrating its barriers.

In two letters written nearly a decade after the novel's appearance, London described his work as "an indictment of individualism" as well as a rebuttal of "the superhuman philosophy of Nietzsche and of modern German ideas."[1] In the latter letter, he relates *The Sea-Wolf* to the same type of critiques contained in both *Martin Eden* and his more politically inclined works, *The War of the Classes*, *Revolution*, and *The Iron*

Heel. For London, the political was always personal. His critique of selfish and brutal individualism is a key feature of all his works, showing him a novelist who has much to say to the contemporary world, a world suffering from the adverse effects of the individualism championed by Ronald Reagan and Margaret Thatcher.

The Sea-Wolf became a great success on publication easily eclipsing *The Call of the Wild*, which appeared in the previous year. Both became London's only works to achieve first place on the newly devised American best-seller list. Most reviews were favorable, but others criticized the work as little better than a "dime-novel" and condemned the romantic scenes between Maud and Humphrey in the latter part of the book.[2] However, London wished to demonstrate the redeeming powers of love both on the personal and political levels. It was an impossible goal to achieve but one he attempted in *The Sea-Wolf* with mixed results. Naturally, as the author's reputation grew and changed over the years, he would become ideologically transmitted as an adventure writer for adolescents, his political relevance generally ignored by most critics. The film industry became one of the mechanisms used to deny London's political ideas in the various versions made of his work.

Both during and after his lifetime, several film versions were made of Jack London's work.[3] However, his 1904 maritime novel, *The Sea-Wolf* particularly attracted filmmakers in the twentieth century. At least eight versions were filmed; the screenplay here is the "final version" of October 22, 1940. During 1913 the Balboa Amusement Company and Bosworth Incorporated produced rival versions, the last directed by and starring Hobart Bosworth in the role of Wolf Larsen. Two other versions appeared during the silent era—George Melford's 1920 Paramount-Artcraft production and the 1926 film featuring Ralph W. Ince who portrayed Larsen. The year 1930 saw the first sound version directed by Alfred Santell and starring silent film adventure star Milton Sills who died of a heart attack soon after completing the role. The rights then passed to David O. Selznick who then sold them to Warner Brothers who hoped to remake the film starring Paul Muni. During the 1930s the actor was establishing a reputation as one of cinema's most distinguished character actors appearing in Warner biopics such as *The Story of Louis Pasteur* (1936), *The Life of Emile Zola* (1937) as well as playing a diversely mixed group of characters such as Wang Lung in *The Good Earth* (1937). Muni had also previously starred in many Warner Brothers social dramas such as *I Am a Fugitive from a Chain Gang* (1932) and *Black Fury* (1935). They were the type of films which would bring charges of "premature anti-Fascism" against socially con-

From Novel to Film   xix

scious talents in the dark days of the Hollywood blacklist a decade later, a movement that effectively ruined Muni's screen career. Authenticity and realism were important features in any film Muni appeared in. The extremely conscientious actor insisted on his choice of roles and took special care in personally choosing the makeup needed for his parts in terms of historical accuracy. But in a November 1, 1937, letter to his agent Muni stressed his unwillingness to appear in a film version of *The Sea-Wolf* that would differ considerably from the original source material. He also wished to collaborate on the screenplay and suggested the pedestrian Mervyn Le Roy as director who "properly guided on story problems . . . is capable of turning out a fine film."[4]

The studio then offered the role of George Leach (which was considerably enlarged in comparison to the book) to one of its star contract players, George Raft. But Raft regarded the role as little better than a bit part and added Leach to the many stimulating roles he rejected during his career such as Roy Earle in *High Sierra* and Sam Spade in *The Maltese Falcon* (both 1941).[5] The company finally made the film featuring Edward G. Robinson in the title role of the most well-known and extant version—the 1941 Warner Brothers production.

Other versions followed. Warner Brothers actually remade the film as a 1950 western, *Barricade*, with no credit given to its original source. Allied Artists filmed *The Sea Wolf* under the title, *Wolf Larsen* in 1958. In 1971 a German-Austrian, French, Rumanian coproduction appeared under the title of *Der Seewolf*. A Rumanian two-part film version appeared in the following year followed by an Italian production, *The Legend of the Sea Wolf*, in 1975 starring Chuck Connors as Wolf Larsen. The most recent version appeared in 1993 featuring Charles Bronson as Wolf Larsen and Christopher Reeve as Humphrey Van Weyden. Other productions are likely to appear in the future since London's original novel lends itself to cinematic recreation as an adventure story.

However, it is the Warner Brothers version that is the best known and most imaginatively constructed of all the films that have survived. Produced by one of the most notable studios in the Golden Age of the Hollywood system, *The Sea Wolf* benefited from all the advantages which French film critic André Bazin once termed "the genius of the system." It featured major stars and actors such as Edward G. Robinson, Ida Lupino, John Garfield, Barry Fitzgerald, John Garfield, Alexander Knox, and Howard Da Silva. Michael Curtiz directed the film, produced by Hal Wallis, shot by one of the most professional directors of photography working in the system Sol Polito, with set design by Anton Grot, and featuring a music score by Erich Wolfgang Korngold.

All of these names had distinguished records within the Hollywood studio system resulting in *The Sea Wolf* becoming more of a group collaboration than the individual product of its original author, although he was featured prominently in the opening credits. Curtiz had previously directed Errol Flynn costume adventures such as *Captain Blood* (1935), *The Charge of the Light Brigade* (1936), *The Private Lives of Elizabeth and Essex* (1939), and *The Sea Hawk* (1940) as well as codirecting *The Adventures of Robin Hood* (1939). Curtiz was later to direct other Hollywood classics such as *Yankee Doodle Dandy* (1942), *Casablanca* (1943), and the *film noir* melodrama *Mildred Pierce* (1945), as well as Hollywood's problematic tribute to its wartime Soviet ally *Mission to Moscow* (1943). Curtiz had also directed Paul Muni in *Black Fury* and John Garfield in *Four Daughters* as well as James Cagney in one of the late 1930s socially conscious gangster movies, *Angels with Dirty Faces*. Curtiz was a highly prolific director and a problematic case in terms of discerning any personal signature within his films according to the individualist tenets of Andrew Sarris's definition of the auteur theory.[6] In this particular case, the significance of *The Sea Wolf* owes less to its particular director and more to a complex association of historically determined factors and union of significant talents happening at the time, the most instrumental of which was screenwriter Robert Rossen. All worked within a studio that attempted some limited, yet nonetheless interesting, social commentaries within its films.

Director of photography Sol Polito established his reputation by his superb black and white cinematography on many Warner Brothers films during the 1930s and 1940s. He had worked with Curtiz on *The Charge of the Light Brigade, The Adventures of Robin Hood, The Private Lives of Elizabeth and Essex,* and *The Sea Hawk,* as well as socially conscious dramas such as *I Am a Fugitive from a Chain Gang* and gangster films such as *G-Men* (1935). Anton Grot worked as art director on many Warner Brothers films during this era such as *Little Caesar* (1932), *20,000 Years in Sing Sing* (1933), *Captain Blood, The Life of Emile Zola* (1937), *They Made Me a Criminal, Juarez* (both 1939), *The Private Lives of Elizabeth and Essex, The Sea Hawk,* and *Mildred Pierce*. Finally, special effects contributor Byron Haskin would later direct science fiction classics such as *The War of the Worlds* (1953), *Robinson Crusoe on Mars* (1964), and *The Power* (1968).

Unlike its predecessors, the Warner Brothers version of *The Sea Wolf* benefited from being part of a carefully planned and marketed studio strategy lending itself to be promoted under one of the many genres that the studio specialized in. Dealing with the conflict between brutal sea captain, Wolf Larsen, and overcivilized, undeveloped male, Humphrey Van Weyden, the story immediately lent itself to those masculine clashes within many of the studio's adventure genres whether western, gangster, or musical. However, what is most remarkable about the Warner Brothers production is its relationship to a pertinent historical era and studio. Warner Brothers was a studio that explicitly supported the New Deal policies of Franklin D. Roosevelt, designed to ease the harsh nature of the Great Depression in the 1930s. Although Warner Brothers never made revolutionary films with radical solutions, it was unique among all the Hollywood studios in at least recognizing the grim realities of its historical era rather than presenting its audiences with the glossy Art Deco escapism of MGM or the Astaire-Rogers dancing romances of R.K.O. Its gritty gangster films featuring contract players such as James Cagney, Humphrey Bogart, and Edward G. Robinson breathed the air of the harsh circumstances of the decade even if the solutions presented were as socially unrealistic as the escapist worlds of MGM, Paramount, and others.

As many articles in 1970s issues of the respected film journal *The Velvet Light Trap* reveal, the studio was highly tuned to contemporary developments and often molded its films to reflect them—even costume adventure films such as *The Sea Hawk* (1940) featuring Errol Flynn with Flora Robson repeating her role as Queen Elizabeth from *Fire Over England* (1937) and concluding the film with a resounding address highly relevant to an England fighting alone against the Nazis.

The Sea Wolf's genesis and reception involved the presence of many talents associated with Hollywood's radical fringe, many of whom would face blacklisting and harassment in the next decade. Abem Finkel and Norman Reilly Raine worked on the temporary script outline. Both writers had written some socially conscious Warner Brothers films such as *Black Legion* (1937) and *Each Dawn I Die* (1939). The final screenplay was drafted by Robert Rossen who was involved in Hollywood radicalism in the 1930s and would eventually face blacklisting until agreeing to cooperate with the House Committee on Un-American Activities in 1953. Rossen had coscripted *Marked Woman* (1937) with Abem Finkel, a thinly veiled allegorical exposure of women's victimization under capitalism. Many of Rossen's scripts such as his collaborative work *They Won't Forget* (1937) and *Dust Be My Destiny* (1939) dealt with social problems most film depictions of the 1930s era tended to ignore. Both films were produced by Warner Brothers. Studio head

Jack Warner cited both these films as subversive during his testimony before the House Committee on Un-American Activities on October 20, 1947.[7] Although originally subpoenaed to appear before the Committee in 1947, Rossen's appearance was suspended allowing him to direct politically committed films such as the boxing melodrama, *Body and Soul* (1947) and *All the King's Men* (1949). He also worked uncredited on *The Treasure of the Sierra Madre* (1948). In the same year he wrote *The Sea Wolf* screenplay, Rossen cowrote *Out of the Fog*, a gangster melodrama featuring John Garfield as a racketeer, a character almost identical to the Wolf Larsen he opposed as George Leach in *The Sea Wolf*. After "naming names" before the Committee, Rossen's career declined until he returned to critical approval with *The Hustler* (1964) featuring Paul Newman in the acclaimed role of "Fast Eddie," a character contaminated by the same system corrupting all those trapped in the maritime hell Rossen earlier depicted in *The Sea Wolf*.

Rossen obviously recognized the political overtones in Jack London's novel and rewrote it as an allegory of 1930s fascism. The film is more the product of its screenwriter than its director, contradicting conventional interpretations of authorship seeing the director as the main motivating force. While compromised by its presence within a Hollywood system promoting entertainment, *The Sea Wolf* nevertheless emerged as an allegory of the brutal world of the post-Depression era that would soon become immersed in World War II. By depicting its main character less as London's victimizer-victim of industrial capitalism and more as a thinly disguised European dictator, *The Sea Wolf* could use certain historical circumstances allowing talents working within a particular studio system to make a highly compromised, yet relevant allegory for the times.

In his various drafts of the screenplay, Rossen dropped many of the features in the original novel that had become hopelessly dated such as the romantic interlude between Humphrey and Maud on Endevour Island. Furthermore, he placed the novel's original hero into the position of a supporting player choosing instead to elevate a character who played a minor role in the actual novel, rebellious seaman George Leach. The role was enlarged to accommodate John Garfield's contemporary star persona as Warner Brothers' archetypal 1930s proletarian hero. Maud Brewster became Ida Lupino's hard-bitten Ruth Webster, a woman fleeing from both prison and a life of prostitution. Her role was obviously modeled upon her predecessor in Alfred Santell's 1930 film version, prostitute Lorna Marsh. Following Warner Brothers screen patterns, a working-class hero and heroine now come into prominence totally eclipsing Jack London's original upper-middle-class characters Humphrey and Maud who obviously would not gain audience sympathies of a different generation.

Although the completed film bears many traces of Rossen's political critique, it is a pale shadow of the writer's original intentions. Although the studio dropped certain embarrassing elements such as romantic scenes 310–12 between Leach and Ruth when they escape from the boat, other deleted parts reveal a much harder political edge to the overall conception. In his opening appearance John Garfield's Leach bears less of a resemblance to any character from 1900 and more to a Depression-era heroic "Forgotten Man" as represented in films such as *I Am a Fugitive from a Chain Gang* (1932), *Heroes for Sale* (1933), and the unemployed veteran in the finale of *Gold Diggers of 1933*. When Larsen speaks to his crew on the day after the fight in the forecastle, he exhibits anger at the "fat shipowners" who offered him the position of skipper of the sealing fleet, now occupied by his vengeful brother, Death Larsen. Wolf Larsen explicitly states that the reason for his refusal was his unwillingness to become "just another cog in the machine" and his refusal to be bought like his brother. Death Larsen's ship, the *Macedonia*, is described as a "modern" vessel symbolizing a new industrial order which has made Larsen and his men redundant figures in the maritime economy. When Larsen speaks of his anger at the company owning the *Macedonia*, he looks in the direction of Van Weyden. A reverse shot reveals the formerly privileged representative of the upper class reacting to Larsen's comments. Larsen then states the obvious consequences to his crew: "Ten years from now . . . by 1910 they'll cover the face of the sea . . . sweeping everything before them . . . and people like us won't be able to find a vessel like the 'Ghost' to ship on . . . we'll be on the beaches livin' off garbage."

He then appeals to the greed of his men by speaking of the riches they will gain by stealing. This speech is not just too political even for Warner Brothers but depicts Larsen and his men as a darker version of Robin Hood and his Merry Men. (Ironically, Michael Curtiz had codirected Errol Flynn's technicolor swashbuckler, *The Adventures of Robin Hood*, for Warner Brothers in 1938!) Many of the philosophic exchanges between Larsen and Van Weyden ended up on the cutting-room floor because the dialogue held up the action. However, the dynamic nature of many Rossen political speeches were too highly charged and relevant to a Depression era the audience had actually lived through. Thus, the producers made certain they would never appear on the cinema screen. Like other film adaptations of Jack London's work, much effort went into making the final screen product "harmless entertainment."[8] But even studio self-censorship could not prevent certain relevant implications from appearing on the screen.

It is hard to believe that talents such as Robinson, Garfield, and Lupino were unaware of the film's implications. In fact, the advance studio publicity quotes Ida Lupino as drawing relevant political parallels. According to an article entitled, *"The Sea Wolf* Shows Dictator Methods Afloat," Lupino comments that had the film been set on land rather than at sea, "it would pass as current history." She notes that Robinson's character "would have been called The Dictator instead of Wolf Larsen" dominating the "have-nots" (played by herself and John Garfield) who are "slaves to conditions we cannot fight." It is interesting to note that both Lupino and Garfield play working-class characters in this film and are regarded as more important than the original hero, Humphrey Van Weyden, who now becomes a subordinate player in the drama. Lupino then continued her history lesson:

> Alexander Knox plays the idealist, Van Weyden, whom the dictator cannot understand. Knox represents the democracies.
> Francis McDonald, first mate, who carries out Larsen's orders, is a perfect minister of foreign affairs.
> *The Sea Wolf* is the story of a man who believes only in brute force. He is so firm in belief in his own ideas that he despises all who disagree with him. He preaches the doctrine of intolerance. He flaunts the notion that democracy is anything but weakness.
> I hope my comparison with history holds to the end. Wolf Larsen sinks with his ship."[9]

Most of the people involved with the film would later come under suspicion by the reactionary forces of McCarthyism in the post–World War II era. Robinson was accused of being a Communist by *Red Channels*, published by the American Business Consultants in 1947, which claimed to identify 151 show business subversive threats to the American Way of Life. The original *Golden Boy* of Clifford Odets's drama, John Garfield, was harassed by the House Committee on Un-American Activities eager to hear him "name names." He eventually died of a heart attack. Both were Jewish, a factor contributing to the postwar anti-Semitism unleashed by the reactionary forces behind the McCarthyite persecutions.[10]

John Garfield was a member of the Committee for the First Amendment against the House Committee on Un-American Activities, an organization whose other leading lights included Humphrey Bogart, Lauren Bacall, Gene Kelly, John Huston, Charles Boyer, Senator Clark Pepper, Sterling Hayden, Helen Keller, and Albert Einstein. Like George Raft, Garfield also turned down the role of Roy Earle in *High Sierra*. But certain factors influenced Garfield's deliberate preference to accept the third lead role of George Leach in *The Sea Wolf*. Garfield wished to participate in the film version of a novel written by one of his favorite writers, Jack London. Warner Brothers had recently prevented him from accepting a loan-out assignment to star in Columbia's *The Adventures of Martin Eden*, which was finally filmed in 1942 with Glenn Ford in the leading role. Garfield was also a friend of scenarist Robert Rossen.[11]

Although Alexander Knox later went on to star in Darryl Zanuck's production of *Wilson* (1944), based upon the president who had taken America into World War I, his career suffered a form of graylisting resulting in his decision to move to Britain later in the 1940s. Knox was also a writer and obviously familiar with the works of Jack London. Howard Da Silva bravely refused to inform in 1951 and suffered over ten years of isolation from his movie career. Although Michael Curtiz and Ida Lupino remained unscathed during the blacklist era, their Jewish background would have tuned them to recognizing relevant implications concerning *The Sea Wolf*'s allegorical representation of the European situation prior to Pearl Harbor. Lupino later went on to become a director of films such as *Outrage* (1951), *The Hitch-Hiker* (1953), and *The Bigamist* (1953)—films dealing with female victimization under capitalism.

The Warner Brothers *The Sea Wolf* is not Jack London's *The Sea-Wolf*. It is a work which bears little relation to its original source on the formal level. But far from dismissing it from consideration, it is better to recognize it for what it is and appreciate it accordingly. Film versions must always differ from their literary originals to be effective cinematically. The two mediums are different. What is also important is recognizing any adaptation attempting to reflect the concerns of its era by transmitting it in a version which has to be different. *The Sea Wolf* is one such example. However, Rossen's screenplay actually works in highlighting the radical politics in the original source material.

Notes

1. See Jack London to Philo M. Buck Jr., November 5, 1912, and Jack London to H. E. Kelsey, August 3, 1915, in *The Letters of Jack London, Volume Three: 1913–1916*, eds. Earle Labor, Robert C. Leitz III, and I. Milo Shepard (Stanford, CA: Stanford Univ. Press, 1988), 1096, 1439.
2. See Jack London, *The Sea-Wolf*, edited with an introduction by John Sutherland (London: Oxford Univ. Press, 1992), xxxiv.
3. See Tony Williams, *Jack London: The Movies* (Los Angeles: David Rejl, 1992) for relevant information concerning films made up to the time of publication.
4. Rudy Behlmer, ed. *Inside Warner Brothers: 1935–1951* (New York: Viking, 1985), 131–32.
5. See Behlmer, *Inside Warner Brothers*, 132–33.
6. Andrew Sarris, *The American Cinema* (New York: E. P. Dutton, 1968), 194–96, lists Curtiz amongst the "lightly likeable." For one recent survey of the director's work, see Sidney Rosenzweig, *Casablanca and Other Major Films of Michael Curtiz* (Ann Arbor, MI: UMI Research Press, 1982).
7. See Gordon Kahn, *Hollywood on Trial* (New York: Boni and Goer, 1948), 13.
8. See Tony Williams, "Clarence E. Shurtleff Presents Jack London, 1919–1921," *Wide Angle* 15.3 (1993): 58–72.
9. Quoted from advance studio publicity from the Warner Brothers Archives, Special Collections, University of Wisconsin-Madison.
10. For evidence of anti-Semitism as a significant feature of the postwar McCarthyite reaction, see Victor S. Navasky, *Naming Names* (London: John Calder, 1982), 109–21; Larry Ceplair and Steven Englund, *The Inquisition in Hollywood: Politics in the Film Community, 1930–1960* (Berkeley: Univ. of California Press, 1983), 289, 317–18.
11. See George Morris, "John Garfield," in *An Illustrated History of the Movies* (New York: Harvest, 1977), 73. For further information on John Garfield, see Larry Swindell, *Body and Soul: The Story of John Garfield* (New York: Morrow, 1975); Howard Gelman, *The Films of John Garfield*, introduction by Abraham Polonsky (Seacaucus, NJ: Citadel Press, 1975); James Beaver, *John Garfield: His Life and Films* (South Brunswick, NJ: A. S. Barnes, 1978); and Robert Sklar, *City Boys* (Princeton, NJ: Princeton Univ. Press, 1992).

Jack London's
The Sea Wolf

Cast of Characters
"Wolf" Larsen: *Captain of the "Ghost"*
Humphrey Van Weyden: *Writer*
George Leach: *A young sailor*
Johnson: *An older sailor, Leach's friend*
Ruth Webster: *Escaped convict aboard the "Ghost"*
Svenson: *Hunter and first mate*
Smoke: *One of the hunters*
Harrison: *One of the sailors*
Louie: *Ship's doctor*
Cooky: *The cockney cook*

Bits
Man in the saloon, a policeman,
Barbary Coast woman entertainer,
stranger on ferryboat,
two detectives

Atmosphere
Barbary Coast types (1900),
ferryboat passengers,
sailors, hunters, etc.

Cast

"Wolf" Larsen *Edward G. Robinson*
Ruth Webster *Ida Lupino*
George Leach *John Garfield*
Humphrey Van Weyden *Alexander Knox*
Dr. Prescott ("Louie") *Gene Lockhart*
Cooky *Barry Fitzgerald*
Johnson *Stanley Ridges*
Young Sailor *David Bruce*
Svenson *Francis McDonald*
Harrison *Howard Da Silva*
Smoke *Frank Lackteen*

Production

Director: Michael Curtiz
Executive Producer: Hal Wallis
Associate Producer: Henry Blanke
Screenplay: Robert Rossen,
from the novel by Jack London
Director of Photography: Sol Polito
Art Director: Anton Grot
Dialogue Director: Jo Graham
Editor: George Amy
Sound: Oliver S. Garretson
Special Effects: Byron Haskin
and H. F. Koenenkamp
Makeup: Percy Westmore

FADE IN

1. MEDIUM SHOT   A FOG SHROUDED COBBLESTONE STREET
   SHOOTING AT STREET LEVEL

Through the fog in the background we occasionally catch glimpses of the spars of sailing vessels anchored at the wharves. A horse and cart rumbles over the street, making, for an instant, an unholy clatter, which added to the SOUNDS of fog horns coming in from the Bay, gives the scene an eerie effect. The wheels of the cart fill the screen, then disappear from sight, taking with them their clatter. For an instant the street is deathly quiet, then faintly a sharp, staccato sound is HEARD, like the sound of a man's feet. The SOUND comes closer and with its immanence appears the indistinct figure of a man, running as fast as he can. He heads straight for the CAMERA, coming so close until we see only his feet. He stops quickly, as the sharp, quick blast of a police whistle is HEARD, then turns and dashes sharply out of scene. The CAMERA HOLDS for an instant on the foggy street which has again become quiet save for an insistent blowing of the whistle.

CUT TO:

2. MEDIUM SHOT   TENEMENT HOUSE DOORWAY[1]
   as the man who has been running suddenly finds shelter in its shadows. The dim gas light of a street lamp cuts through the shadows and illumines his face as he stands there breathing heavily. He is a swarthy, intense looking man of about twenty-seven. His name is GEORGE LEACH. In his eyes is a haunted

look. He flattens himself against the door jamb, stays there for a few seconds, then peers cautiously out along the street.

3. LONG SHOT   THE STREET
    The fog has become so dense that it is difficult to see more than a few feet. What little visibility is left discloses the fact that the street is quite deserted.

4. CLOSE SHOT   LEACH
    as his eyes sweep the other side of the street, suddenly he puts up the collar of his coat and steps out of the shadows of the doorway. CAMERA TRUCKS with him, then HOLDS ON his disappearing figure until the fog envelopes it and hides it from our sight. After a while the fog thins and dissolves into clouds of tobacco smoke as the CAMERA MOVES INTO A:

5. CLOSE SHOT   A BLONDE, HARD-LOOKING WOMAN
    dressed in the typical spangled costume that entertainers wore on the Barbary Coast in the year 1900. She is singing a sentimental song of the period as the CAMERA DRAWS BACK and PANS:

6. MEDIUM PANNING SHOT   THE SALOON[2]
    CAMERA PICKS UP the various types who inhabit the place, as OVER SHOT comes the raucous voice of the woman . . . sailors, prostitutes, confidence men, cut-throats and murderers. It is not a pretty picture that the CAMERA paints, for it leaves one indelible impression . . . complete degradation. It finally COMES TO REST ON:

7. MEDIUM CLOSE   THE DOORS
   as they spring open and Leach enters. He stands there for a moment, surveying his surroundings. As he does so, a man starts out the door, collides with him, apparently accidentally. Quick as a flash, Leach grabs the man's hand, which is in his pocket.

   > **LEACH:**
   > If you find anything in there,
   > brother, I'll share it with you.

   The man looks at him, withdraws his hand hastily, curses under his breath at him and disappears. Leach looks after him, smiles and starts to walk towards the bar.

8. MEDIUM CLOSE   AT BAR
   as Leach approaches. He takes his place next to a group of three men. Suddenly, his attention is attracted by the sight of the man in the middle, a great blond Scandinavian of about forty whose apparel indicates that he is a sailor. His name is JOHNSON. He is surrounded by two men. One of them is a voluble, crafty little man, the other a tough, burly sailor named SVENSON.

   > **JOHNSON:**
   > *(he speaks slowly; there is a slight trace of an accent in his speech)*
   > What kind of vessel is it?
   >
   > **SVENSON:**
   > A schooner...bound for the Japanese Coast...
   >
   > **JOHNSON:**
   > What's its cargo?
   >
   > **MAN:**
   > I'm only askin' ye to sail on it...not to buy it.
   >
   > **JOHNSON:**
   > I have been tricked before. What's its cargo?

   The man looks at Svenson rather nervously. He turns to Johnson, speaks quickly.

MAN:
It's a seal hunter...if the catch is good, there'll probably be a bonus in it for you.

JOHNSON:
What's the name of the vessel?

There is a pause.

SVENSON:
The "Ghost."

At the mention of the name, a strange hard look comes into Johnson's eyes. He looks at the two men, then suddenly tries to push his way past them, but his path is blocked by the little man who puts his arms on Johnson's sweater. Slowly Johnson removes the man's arms.

MAN:
Wait a minute, sailor.
(talking quickly)
It's not easy for a sailing man like you to get a berth these days—what with steam cutting down on the size of the crews...

JOHNSON:
Get out of my way!

MAN:
Sixty a month, sailor...that's good pay.

JOHNSON:
If you live to collect it!

MAN:
You got this all wrong.

JOHNSON:[3]
I have heard of this ship...I have also heard of its master. I have spoken to men who have sailed aboard it. The fear that comes into their eyes at the mention of the name "Ghost" or its master "Wolf" Larsen is enough for me. They all look like men who have

come, not from a voyage on the sea, but from a voyage through hell itself.

MAN:
You're not afraid of hard work, are you?

JOHNSON:[4]
No work is hard—if you can still remain a human being while doing it. [From what men say that is not possible aboard the "Ghost."
(pride in his voice)
I am an able seaman...I can still choose the kind of ship I sail on.]
(slowly, with disgust in his voice)
I wouldn't sail aboard a ship like the "Ghost" if she were the only sailing vessel left on the Pacific Ocean.
(he walks away)

As he does so, the man who has been talking nods to Svenson who nods back and quickly follows Johnson. Leach watches this with interest. As Svenson follows Johnson, he is joined by Oarsman No. 1 and Oarsman No. 2 who get up from a table. They walk out into the night. CAMERA HOLDS for an instant on the swinging doors, then PANS QUICKLY BACK TO:

9. MEDIUM CLOSE   AT BAR
as Leach and the man are left there alone. The man keeps looking curiously at Leach whose back is to the bar. He still looks out toward the door. Suddenly the door swings open and a policeman appears. Quick as a flash Leach turns, pulls his cap over his eyes and buries his head on the bar, giving the appearance of a drunken man.

10. REVERSE ANGLE SHOOTING   INTO MIRROR
as we see the policeman stand in the doorway, look around and then go out. The man has noticed this. He moves over to Leach.

11. MEDIUM CLOSE UP   AT BAR   LEACH AND MAN
The man taps him on the shoulder.

MAN:
It's all right, buddy,[5] he's gone.

LEACH:
(lifting his head slowly, pretending innocence)
Who?

MAN:
The copper.

LEACH:
(snarling)
I don't know what you're talking about.

MAN:
(smiling)
All right...forget I said it.
(pauses)
I'll buy you a drink.

LEACH:
(suspiciously)
Why?

MAN:
I don't like to drink alone.[6]

He turns to the bartender and nods. The bartender nods back and turns his back on the men, presumably mixing a drink.

12. REVERSE ANGLE   LEACH   SHOOTING PAST MAN TOWARD BARTENDER
Leach's eyes are riveted on the bartender. It is obvious that the man is trying to hide his view.

MAN:
(to Leach)
Sailor?

LEACH:
I've been on a ship.
(as Leach talks he keeps his eyes riveted on the bartender)

13. WIDER ANGLE
    as the bartender turns and shoves the two glasses in front of them. The man casually throws a coin on the bar and lifts his glass.

    > **MAN:**
    > Well, here's how...

    Leach lifts his glass, then instead of drinking it, suddenly throws its contents in the man's face. The man staggers back, blinded by it, then suddenly makes a lunge for Leach who clips him flush on the jaw and knocks him down. In a flash, he is surrounded by several men who seem to appear from nowhere. Quickly Leach's hand goes to his belt. He half draws a knife from its sheath. Its glint causes the men to stop.

    > **LEACH:**
    > *(his voice deadly)*
    > You don't have to slip me a Mickey to get me on board your boat...I'll ship on the first and the quickest ship out of here.

    DISSOLVE TO:

14. MEDIUM SHOT.   A DORY   NIGHT
    Hidden in the shadows underneath a wharf, its prow tied to one of the poles that supports the wharf. In the boat, through the darkness the figure of several men can be seen. The slapping of the water against the pier is the only SOUND we hear until out of shot comes the creaking SOUND of feet coming down the runway that leads to the floating pier. The men in the boat look up.

15. REVERSE ANGLE   SHOOTING FROM DORY
    as Leach comes down the runway. He stands there for an instant, trying to pierce the darkness, not noticing the boat. Suddenly through the darkness comes a man's voice:

    > **VOICE:**
    > Hey...you...

16. WIDER ANGLE
 as the dory rows up the wharf. Svenson rises in the prow.

> SVENSON:
> You the feller that signed on for the "Ghost"?
> *(Leach nods)*[7]

Leach gets into the boat. Svenson begins to row and the boat moves into the Bay.

17. MEDIUM CLOSE   INTERIOR DORY   (PROCESS SHOT)
 as Leach settles himself in the stern. Next to him is seated a man, hunched over, his head buried between his knees. He looks at him curiously. The man makes no motion, but just sways with the motion of the boat.

> LEACH:
> *(to the man at the oars—Svenson)*
> Drunk?

Svenson nods.[8] Suddenly a swell causes the boat to rock violently. As it does so, the man pitches forward and falls to the bottom of the dory. He lies there, as though he were stunned by the fall. Leach bends down and tries to lift him up. He succeeds in turning him over. As he does so, he recoils.

18. CLOSE ANGLE SHOT   LEACH'S ANGLE
 The man lying at the bottom of the boat is Johnson, the sailor we saw in the saloon. His head is a mass of bruises and cuts. A

clot of blood that has dried on his face adds the last gruesome note to his features. The expression on Svenson's face doesn't change. It is still stony and impassive. There is a long silence, broken only by the creak of the oars. Suddenly, o.s., comes the cackling, almost idiotic laugh of a man. Leach looks up. CAMERA SWINGS with his gaze to:

19. MEDIUM CLOSE SHOT   PROW OF THE BOAT
Sitting there with his legs crossed, looking for all the world like an evil dwarf, grinning that strange toothless grin peculiar only to him is COOKY. In his hands he holds a half empty bottle of liquor.

> COOKY:
> *(still cackling)*
> Now...I wonder 'ow that 'appened?..
> *(the cackle grows louder and more hysterical)*

CAMERA DRAWS BACK to include the rest of the men in the dory.

> SVENSON:
> *(to Leach, explaining)*
> He's drunk. Don't pay him no mind.

> COOKY:
> *(almost shrieking in his drunken hysteria)*
> 'Ow else d'ye think we can get men to sail on board a 'el ship like the "Ghost"?...D'ye think they're all fools like you are?...

> SVENSON:
> Shut up, Cooky...

> COOKY:
> I won't shut up...let the chills of fear run up 'is spine...like they did mine when I made my first v'yage on board the foulest ship in creation...
> *(he spits in disgust)*
> Ah, ye'll 'ave a fine time aboard the "Ghost."

> SVENSON:
> I won't tell ye again, Cooky!

COOKY:

(ignoring him)

At night ye'll go to sleep prayin' for the mornin' an' during the day ye'll pray for the night...an' there's one thing ye'll pray for most of all...[9] to live to see the day when someone rips with their bare fingers from its livin' body...the cold merciless heart of the beast of the sea that men call "Wolf" Larsen...

SVENSON:

I said—shut up!

He suddenly puts down his oars and turning, hits Cooky a full swinging blow. Cooky slumps down in his seat and is quiet.

20. MEDIUM CLOSE   STERN
as Leach looks about him quickly. Escape is read in his eyes. The man seated directly in front of him notices this. He slowly draws a pistol from his belt and levels it at Leach.[10]

MAN:

(slowly)

If you're thinkin' of breakin' for it, laddie, I'm tellin' ye now, the only way you'll ever make the shore is floatin'...face downward

Leach sits there, his arms gripping tensely the sides of the boat as the man signals to Svenson who begins to row again.

21. MEDIUM SHOT   THE DORY
as it makes its way further out to sea. Suddenly out of shot is HEARD the hoarse, frantic blast of a siren. Svenson begins to row furiously in a frenzied effort to get out of the way. The men look backwards.

22. MEDIUM SHOT   A FERRYBOAT   (MINIATURE)
It moves slowly through the water, occasionally hidden completely by the dense fog that covers the Bay like a shroud. The fog is so thick that the only indication we have of other boats in the Bay is the SOUNDS of their sirens and other fog horns,

which keep up a continual din. The mournful tolling of a bell gives rhythm to the scene. The ferryboat cuts across the stern of the dory, blotting it completely from view.

23. CLOSE SHOT   A LIFE PRESERVER.
On it is the legend:

> **Municipal Ferryboat Co.**
> **San Francisco.**

CAMERA TILTS UP TO:

24. MEDIUM CLOSE   AT FERRYBOAT RAIL   HUMPHREY VAN WEYDEN
He is a slight, studious looking man, dressed in the conservative fashion of the day. Under one of his arms he carries a brief case. He stares straight ahead of him as though trying to pierce he fog. Turning up his collar against the damp air, Van Weyden turns and walks back toward the cabin. The CAMERA HOLDS for an instant on the empty deck until a heavy bank of fog completely obliterates it from view. O.S. comes the mournful wail of a fog horn.

25. to 33. OMITTED[11]

34. MEDIUM SHOT   INTERIOR MAIN CABIN   FERRYBOAT
as Van Weyden enters. It is completely deserted, save for one person, a woman of about twenty-three, who sits in the corner of a bench next to the door. She is reading a newspaper. She looks up quickly as Van Weyden enters, then as quickly does she go back to reading her paper. Van Weyden doesn't pay any particular attention to her, but crosses over to the opposite side of the cabin and seats himself on a bench, opens a book and begins to read.

35. CLOSE SHOT   THE WOMAN
Her beauty is undeniable. It is marred only by a bitter, hard, hunted look that hovers around her eyes. She seems nervous and finds it very difficult to keep her eyes focused on the paper. Every so often, as steps are HEARD on the outside of the deck,

her head jerks quickly...her body stiffens and becomes poised like an athlete about to start off in a race.

36. CLOSE SHOT   VAN WEYDEN   SHOOTING TOWARD WOMAN
He becomes attracted by her strange behavior. He looks up from the book that he is reading and stares at her.

37. MEDIUM CLOSE   WOMAN   SHOOTING TOWARD VAN WEYDEN
as she realizes he is staring at her.

> **WOMAN:**
> *(the word comes like a sudden explosion)*
> Yes?[12]
>
> **VAN WEYDEN:**
> *(self-consciously)*
> I beg your pardon.

He buries his head in the book. She stares at him, then turns her head away. Her hand begins to wipe away the fog that has dimmed the window, next to which she is seated. At first it seems like an automatic gesture, then suddenly it assumes a frantic air. Into her eyes comes a look of fright.

38. MEDIUM CLOSE   EXTERIOR   DECK
as two heavy-set men appear on the deck. They stare intently at everyone they meet. Their eyes shift constantly, alertly. They have the look of the hunters about them. Suddenly they stop. One of them nods in the direction of the cabin, the other nods acquiescence. They both start toward the cabin.

39. MEDIUM SHOT   INTERIOR CABIN
as the woman springs to her feet. She makes as though to go to the door, then thinks better of it. Van Weyden looks up at her again. She paces up and down like a caged animal, then suddenly notices Van Weyden. Quickly, she moves over to him and sits next to him.

40. MEDIUM CLOSE   BENCH   VAN WEYDEN AND WOMAN

Van Weyden stares at her, completely bewildered by her strange behavior. He makes a move as though to draw away from her, but she quickly grasps his arm.

WOMAN:
(her voice is charged with emotion; her eyes plead desperately)
Two men...they're coming in here...They'll ask questions...you'll say you know me...I'm an old friend of yours...my name is
(she fumbles for a moment)
Maud...Maud Webster[13]...We're going to San Francisco to visit some people—some friends—can you remember that...? Maud...Maud Webster

VAN WEYDEN:
(completely bewildered)
But...

WOMAN:
(desperately)
Please...please.

She looks around quickly. The door starts opening. She turns to Van Weyden.

WOMAN:
What's your name?

VAN WEYDEN:
Van Weyden...Humphrey Van Weyden.

> **WOMAN:**
> *(repeating it)*
> Humphrey Van Weyden...I'll remember it.

41. MEDIUM CLOSE   AT CABIN DOOR
    as the two men enter. They look around for an instant; then their eyes focus on the two people sitting there. The first man looks at the other as though seeking corroboration. The second man nods. They begin to walk over.

42. MEDIUM CLOSE   VAN WEYDEN AND THE WOMAN

    > **WOMAN:**
    > *(as the SOUND of their approaching footsteps is heard)*
    > Talk to me...say anything...please...

43. WIDER ANGLE
    as the two men approach the bench. They stand there looking down at Van Weyden and the woman. There is a moment of complete silence. Slowly Van Weyden rises to his feet.

    > **VAN WEYDEN:**
    > Yes?
    >
    > **1ST MAN:**
    > *(pointing to the woman who still has remained seated)*
    > This woman?
    >
    > **VAN WEYDEN:**
    > *(quickly)*
    > What about her?
    >
    > **1ST MAN:**
    > Is she with you?
    >
    > **VAN WEYDEN:**
    > I fail to see why I have to answer any of your questions.

The man's answer is to reach into his pocket and show Van Weyden a police badge.

2ND MAN:
Before you say anything, sir, I should like to remind you that it's a criminal offense to aid an escaped convict.

VAN WEYDEN:
(an astonished note in his voice)
An escaped convict?[14]

From his pocket the second man takes a folded handbill. Van Weyden opens it slowly and looks at it. As he does so, the woman rises and looks over his shoulder.
INSERT: THE HANDBILL   (BEARING A PHOTOGRAPH OF THE WOMAN)
Above it:

ATTENTION ALL POLICE OFFICERS
Escaped from Lyndale Reformatory for Women
And underneath the photograph, the legend:
Ruth Brewster

44.   TIGHT GROUP SHOT
as Van Weyden holds the handbill. The woman looks at his face, then at the others

RUTH:
(with a slightly forced laugh)
Funny, isn't it? the woman looks just like me...doesn't she...?
(she fumbles for the name a moment)
Humphrey?

There is a silence.

RUTH:
(she talks frantically)
It's lucky I'm with you...otherwise[15] I guess these men would arrest me...and you'd have to come to the police station and go through all sorts of trouble explaining to convince them that...

Her voice trails off as she notices there is no response from Van Weyden.

> **VAN WEYDEN:**
> I'm sorry, miss. There's nothing I can do...the law.
>
> **RUTH:**
> *(bitterly)*
> That's right...the law.
> *(she talks to Van Weyden, mimicking the officer)*
> I want to remind you that it's a criminal offense...
>
> **1ST DETECTIVE:**
> *(taking hold of her arm)*
> All right...that'll be enough. You'll stay here in this cabin until we get to San Francisco...

Ruth suddenly twists out of the detective's grip and dashes out of the cabin, slamming the door behind her. The detectives start after her. Van Weyden stands there for an instant looking after them, then stuffing the handbill in his pocket, follows them.

45. MEDIUM CLOSE   RUTH
    as she runs along the deck, brushing astonished people out of her way.

46. MEDIUM CLOSE   THE TWO MEN
    as they run after her. One of them suddenly stops and goes off in another direction.

47. MEDIUM CLOSE   RUTH
    as she starts clambering up a ladder leading to the upper deck. As she reaches the top step, she suddenly stops. There on the upper deck is one of the detectives awaiting her. She looks down. The other detective is at the bottom of the ladder. Suddenly she climbs over the railing and poises herself, ready to jump.

48. ANGLE SHOT   SHOOTING DOWN STEPS
    Van Weyden stands behind the detective who has started up the ladder, but who has stopped dead in his tracks at her action.

VAN WEYDEN:
(shouting up, terror filling his face)
Don't!...Don't...you mustn't...[16]

Before he can finish his sentence, the boat suddenly swerves sharply, throwing Van Weyden off his feet. The siren of the ferryboat begins to SOUND off in short, frantic, desperate whistles.

49. CLOSE SHOT   THE PILOT HOUSE
The pilot and the captain are frantically trying to reverse the boat. The insistent clanging of the engine bell can be HEARD above the roar of the engine as they start to reverse themselves. Both of their faces are tense and white.

50. MEDIUM CLOSE   AN OCEAN LINER
as it emerges out of the sea, seeming to split the fog like a wedge . . . its bow trailing fog wreathes on either side.

51. MEDIUM CLOSE   THE DECK   VAN WEYDEN
as he stands there, along with the others, too horrified by the immanency of what is about to happen to even cry out. Suddenly, a long crash and rending of timber. A woman's agonized scream and the boat lists heavily to one side, as the ocean pours into the breach. In an instant the deck becomes a madhouse.

52. TRUCKING SHOT   VAN WEYDEN
as we follow him through the hysterical crowd trying to get to the ladder. In the b.g. can be seen the crowd fighting each other, tearing away the seats for the precious life preservers. Van Weyden finally succeeds in making his way to the foot of the ladder on which he last saw the girl. He looks up.

53. MEDIUM CLOSE   THE LADDER
It is empty. It hangs torn from its moorings by the impact of the crash, swaying grotesquely in the wind.

54. MEDIUM CLOSE   VAN WEYDEN
He lowers his head for an instant, then buckling on a life preserver, goes toward one of the boats. The scenes that greet him there are of even greater confusion and hysteria. Suddenly the

boat lists even more sharply. The crowd tries desperately to hang on to whatever it can, screaming, yelling. Van Weyden gets caught in the panic of the crowd.

55.   OMITTED[17]

56.   CLOSE SHOT   VAN WEYDEN
as a huge wave sweeps over the deck, blotting the crowd from view and completely filling the screen.

DISSOLVE TO:

57.   LONG SHOT   THE BAY
Through the fog and darkness we can make out a lone figure clinging to a piece of debris.

58.   CLOSER SHOT
It is Van Weyden, panting as though he had just reached it. He tries to hoist himself upwards . . . when suddenly he stops and looks off.

59.   MEDIUM CLOSE   THE OCEAN
Long hair floating on top of the water indicates the presence of a woman.

60.   MEDIUM CLOSE   VAN WEYDEN
As the figure floats by, he reaches out and grabs it . . . the head emerges . . . a look of horror comes into his eyes . . . as he notices that it is Ruth . . . the girl . . . her face already turned blue

by long immersion in the water . . . her eyes wide open in the stare of a drowned person. Desperately, frantically he pulls her toward the log. He hangs there, one arm around the woman . . . the other on the log. Suddenly he hears the sound of ship's bells close by. He looks up.

61. CLOSE SHOT   THE PROW OF A SCHOONER
    The prow of a schooner cuts through the fog. As it comes closer we see dimly outlined its name: THE "GHOST" as OVER SHOT we HEAR:

    > **VAN WEYDEN'S VOICE:**
    > *(hoarsely)*
    > Ahoy, there..."Ghost"...ahoy[18] there..."Ghost"...

    His voice is intermingled with the SOUND of the bells as the hull of the schooner fills the screen and the name "Ghost" looms larger. Through the fog we see the figure of a man appear at the rail of the ship. He throws a lifeline down to Van Weyden who clutches desperately at it as it hits the water, and we

    DISSOLVE TO:

62. MEDIUM SHOT   THE OCEAN[19]   MORNING
    as seen through a porthole. As the waves break in monotonous regularity against the glass, filling it, then washing away, giving the unreal and distorted quality that only water against glass can give.

CAMERA PULLS BACK TO:

63. MEDIUM CLOSE SHOT   A SHIP'S GALLEY
    revealing the fact that we have seen the waves through a glass. The SHOT is distorted and out of focus. All the objects in it are indistinguishable, and made even more so by the pitch and roll of the ship. OVER SHOT is HEARD something that resembles a great many gongs and yet is as completely unreal as the rest of the scene. Slowly the SHOT goes into focus.

64. MEDIUM CLOSE SHOT   A SHIP'S GALLEY
    It is a dirty, greasy, confined room below decks. On one side is a gas range. Hanging along the walls is a collection of frying pans and pots. The roll of the ship causes them to bang against each other, in a discordant, jangling symphony that seems to fit in with the noise of the sea and the incessant creaking of the wooden floor. But now the noises are real. The room is quite deserted.

CAMERA PANS TO:

65. CLOSE SHOT   VAN WEYDEN
    as he lies in a bunk. As he slowly opens is eyes, a violent roll of the boat almost pitches him from his bunk. He grabs on to the sides, desperately. Then slowly he looks about him. He puts his hands to his ears as though trying to shut out the noises. Gradually he sits up. He turns and looks out the porthole.

66. THE OCEAN   FROM THE PORTHOLE
    It seems to rush by with ever increasing speed. There is no sign of land anywhere.

67. MEDIUM CLOSE   VAN WEYDEN
    Again, he looks about the galley. Its emptiness seems terrifying. Suddenly, he shouts out.

    VAN WEYDEN:
    Hey, there!! Somebody...is anyone here?

    A silence . . . broken only by the creaking of the boards. Beads

of sweat indicating his terror show on his forehead. Again he
cries out.

> **VAN WEYDEN:**
> Is anyone here?!...

Again there is silence. He looks about him, panic-stricken,
then suddenly makes a mad dash for the stairs leading to the
deck.

68. CLOSE SHOT   HATCHWAY
    as Van Weyden emerges from the galley. He stands there for an
    instant, surveying his surroundings and clinging to a corner
    cabin for support against the pitching of the boat. He looks
    about him quickly, as though searching for some visible sign of
    life. Then suddenly his eyes focus directly ahead of him.

69. LONG SHOT   REVERSE ANGLE   SHOOTING OVER VAN WEY-
    DEN'S SHOULDER TOWARD PROW OF BOAT
    From Van Weyden's angle, we see in the distance a group of
    sailors gathered around in a semi-circle. Overhead on the
    bridge, overlooking the scene, silhouetted against the white
    mast, is the figure of a man. Suddenly the man turns his back
    to the scene.

70. CLOSE SHOT   THE BACK OF THE MAN
    It looms large and forbidding, almost filling the screen. Then it
    starts to move away from the CAMERA. As it does, we see that
    we are on:

71. MEDIUM SHOT   THE SHIP'S BRIDGE
    The figure of the man moves toward the end of the bridge, sud-
    denly stops and looks down, then turns and comes back into
    CAMERA, revealing for the first time the face of WOLF LARSEN.

72. MEDIUM CLOSE   WOLF LARSEN
    The most significant thing about him is the impression of
    strength he gives. It is much more than a physical one. It seems
    to be an inner strength. It is in his eyes, his voice, his move-
    ments. He exudes authority, decisiveness, and above all from

the way he looks at the others, great contempt. He looks down again, his hands gripping the rail as though in his rage he would break it. As he does so, the CAMERA, following his gaze

PAN QUICKLY TO:

73. ANGLE SHOT   SHOOTING DOWN FROM BRIDGE
Stretched out on the hatch is a heavily bearded man. He lies face upwards, his eyes closed, apparently unconscious, yet his mouth is open and his breast heaves, spasmodically. One gets the impression that the man is suffocating. A sailor, quite methodically lifts a bucket from the side of the ship, walks over to the man and sluices it over the prostrate man. Then just as methodically, he drops the bucket over the side again. A few men, apparently not sailors, lean against the rail, nonchalantly looking on.

CAMERA SWINGS TO:

74. MEDIUM CLOSE SHOT   VAN WEYDEN
Van Weyden, who has by this time edged his way into the circle, stares horror-stricken at the scene. He turns to Harrison, a burly sailor, who is standing next to him.

> **VAN WEYDEN:**[20]
> That man lying on the deck...?
>
> **HARRISON:**
> *(casually)*
> That's the first mate...I think he's dying.
>
> **VAN WEYDEN:**
> Dying?
>
> **HARRISON:**
> Yes...He's always had a weak heart. I guess all the rum he lapped up in 'Frisco did him in this time. The Old Man'll be awful mad if he croaks...good first mates are hard to find.

A look of horror comes over Van Weyden's face.

VAN WEYDEN:
But nobody even seems to care...they act as though his death were a matter of course.

HARRISON:
(shrugging)
Well, mister, on board this ship...you might say it is.

Van Weyden looks at him for an instant, then suddenly starts forward.

75. MEDIUM CLOSE   AT BRIDGE SHOOTING UP TOWARDS LARSEN
as Van Weyden approaches Wolf Larsen. He stands there for an instant, almost as though he were afraid to approach him. Suddenly, Larsen looks down and notices him. He stands there looking at him, without saying a word.

VAN WEYDEN:
I'm the man who was picked up out of the Bay. I'm deeply grateful.

Larsen doesn't answer. He just stands there and looks at Van Weyden. There is an awkward pause. Van Weyden is about to speak again when suddenly the dying man begins to go into the convulsions of death. His fists beat a tattoo upon the deck, his breath comes faster and faster. Van Weyden turns and looks at him.

76. WIDER ANGLE
as the group of men who have been hanging around the rail draw closer and form a semi-circle about the man. It is as though they were witnessing a fight. And a fight it is . . . between life and death.

77. PANNING SHOT   AROUND THE SHIP
as each sailor looks up from his work towards the semi-circle. It is as though a signal had been set off. Their faces grow even more bitter.

78. MEDIUM GROUP SHOT   THE SEMI-CIRCLE
The sailor who has been dumping the bucket of water into the

dying man's face suddenly stops his swing in mid-air. The fight is over, the muscles relax, the head stops rolling, and a sigh, as of profound relief, escapes from the dying man's lips. Then he is still. The sailor bends down, then looks upward at Larsen

> **SAILOR:**
> He's dead, sir.

There is a silence.

79. CLOSE SHOT   LARSEN
    The clouds of anger that have been gathering on his face suddenly break loose into the storm that they have been foreshadowing.

    > **LARSEN**
    > *(repeating after him, bitterly)*
    > He's dead, sir.
    > *(his words crackle with anger)*
    > My mate is dead...
    > *(he looks down at the dead man)*
    > You dirty, drunken sot...you died too easy. The rum you swilled should have first withered your limbs ...rotted away at your flesh...eaten out your eyes...

80. CLOSE SHOT   VAN WEYDEN
    as he stands horrified at this cursing of a dead man.

    > **VAN WEYDEN:**
    > *(a note of horror in his voice)*
    > The man is dead, sir!

81. CLOSE SHOT   LARSEN[21]

    > **LARSEN:**
    > Man...?
    > *(he says the words with as much contempt as he can possibly muster)*
    > That's not a man any longer...that's just a lump of rum-soaked flesh...

82. REVERSE ANGLE   SHOOTING FROM BRIDGE
    as Larsen turns away from Van Weyden to the group of men who still stand in a semi-circle about the dead man.

    > **LARSEN:**
    > Svenson!!

    One of the men steps forward.

    > **LARSEN:**
    > Get your palm and needle and sew the beggar up. You'll find some old canvas in the sail locker.
    >
    > **SVENSON:**
    > What'll I put on his feet, sir?
    >
    > **LARSEN:**
    > We'll see to that.
    > *(he turns to Cooky, who has been hovering about)*
    > Cooky!! Go below and fill a sack with coal.
    > *(Cooky quickly goes toward the galley. Larsen turns back towards the men)*
    > Any of you fellers got a Bible or a prayer book?
    > *(a short laugh is his answer. He shouts off scene)*
    > Hey!! Any of you fellers got a Bible?

83. PANNING SHOT   THE CREW
    Their answer is a stolid, sullen silence.

84. MEDIUM GROUP SHOT
    as Larsen turns to Van Weyden.

    > **LARSEN:**
    > You look like you might know a prayer or two by heart. As a matter of fact, you've got a preacher's look about you. What's your name?
    >
    > **VAN WEYDEN:**
    > Van Weyden...Humphrey Van Weyden.
    >
    > **LARSEN:**
    > It even sounds like a preacher's name.
    > *(the men laugh)*

VAN WEYDEN:
I'm a writer.

LARSEN:
What do you write about?

VAN WEYDEN:
Whatever I see.

LARSEN:
Is this the first time you ever saw a man die?

VAN WEYDEN:
It's the first time I've ever seen such indifference to death.

LARSEN:
You haven't seen enough to be a good writer...this voyage ought to do you a lot of good.

VAN WEYDEN:
(a note of surprise in his voice)
Voyage? What do you mean?

Larsen is silent. Van Weyden looks at him, then looks about at the faces of the men, stonily impassive. His gaze shifts quickly o.s.

85. OMITTED[22]

86. MEDIUM CLOSE   LARSEN AND VAN WEYDEN

VAN WEYDEN:
That's the pilot boat...that one back there, isn't it?[23]

LARSEN:
That's right.

VAN WEYDEN:
It doesn't seem very far off. It shouldn't take very long to put back. I'll pay you whatever you think your delay is worth.
(Larsen doesn't answer. The terror on Van Weyden's face increases)
Don't you intend putting me ashore?

LARSEN:
No, Mr. Van Weyden, I don't.

VAN WEYDEN:
You can't be serious about this?

LARSEN:
Very serious, Mr. Van Weyden. My mate's dead. That leaves me one man short.[24]

VAN WEYDEN:
(his laughter has a slight note of hysteria in it)
There's nothing I can do aboard a ship.

LARSEN:
(looking at him contemptuously)
No...nothing much. You're soft like a woman.

VAN WEYDEN:
(as the word strikes a responsive chord)
Woman?...
(quickly)
The woman...I'd almost forgotten...what about *her*?

LARSEN:
(calling off)
Cooky!

Cooky's head appears in the hatchway like a jack-in-the-box.

COOKY:
'Ere, sir...at yer service, sir. The sack of coal'll be up in a minute, sir.[25]

LARSEN:
What about that woman that we fished up out of the sea?

COOKY:
Oh, she's in a bad w'y, sir. Louie says 'e 'ardly expects 'er to live through the night.

Van Weyden's face drops. A look of pity comes over it.

COOKY:
(continuing)
'Twould be a shame for 'er to pass away...
(drops his eyes and speaks sanctimoniously, sighs)
She's so young...
(his sigh takes on a different meaning)
An' so beautiful...
(he smirks at the two men)
A wench like that could very well liven up the tedshus days of a long v'yage.
(he cackles again)

VAN WEYDEN:
(suddenly, a note of hope still in his voice)
You'll put me off at the next port of call?

LARSEN:
I touch no ports, Mr. Van Weyden.

VAN WEYDEN:
We'll meet other ships that are sailing back...

LARSEN:
I hardly think so, Mr. Van Weyden. The "Ghost" don't sail the regular ships' lanes. You're stuck on board this ship till we touch the port of 'Frisco again.

VAN WEYDEN:
There's such a thing as the law.

LARSEN:
I'm obeying the law, Mr. Van Weyden...the law of the sea, that says anything you find in it is yours to keep.

Larsen looks at him again coldly, appraisingly.

LARSEN:
I guess you can wash dishes and do scullion work. That'll release an able bodied man for able bodied work. You're signed up as cabin boy...$20 a month.

VAN WEYDEN:
What if I refuse?

Larsen smiles wanly as though his refusal were the most absurd thing in the world. He turns and shouts off.

> **LARSEN:**
> You, cabin boy!!

87. MEDIUM CLOSE   LEACH
    as he stands amidst the other sailors. In contrast to the other sailors, where they have a sullen, hang-dog look, his is a defiant one—a slight trace of a smile curls about his lips—a smile that expresses as much defiance as his eyes.

> **LARSEN'S VOICE:**
> *(o.s.)*
> Come up here!!

He looks around at the other sailors, then slowly and deliberately starts walking toward Larsen.

88. WIDER ANGLE
    as Leach approaches and stands in front of Larsen. There is a slight pause as the two men size each other up. A slightly amused smile comes over Larsen's face, as though in anticipation of what is about to happen.

> **LARSEN:**
> What's your name?
>
> **LEACH:**
> George Leach.
>
> **LARSEN:**
> *(sharply)*
> Sir!!
>
> **LEACH:**
> *(slowly)*
> Sir.
>
> **LARSEN:**
> You ever ship on a schooner, before?

LEACH:
(quickly)
No, sir.

LARSEN:
Who signed you?

LEACH:
I wasn't interested in the man's name.
(he pauses deliberately)
Sir!!

LARSEN:
Did you get any advance money?

LEACH:
I didn't have time to wait for it.
(again he pauses)
Sir...

LARSEN:
You must have been in an awful hurry to get on board.
(Leach doesn't answer—suddenly)
What do the police have on you back in 'Frisco?

LEACH:
(his eyes blazing)
That's a dirty lie—! Nobody's got nothing on me—I can prove it—

LARSEN:
(laughing)
You give yourself away too easy, Leach. You ought to learn to control that temper of yours.[26]
(he looks at him appraisingly)
You're not a cabin boy anymore, Leach—
(he nods in the direction of Van Weyden)
Our literary friend here has taken your job away. You're promoted. You're now a boat puller.
(he turns to Svenson who has been busy sewing up the sack in which the dead man has been placed)
Svenson, what do you know about navigation?

SVENSON:
(looking up)
Nothing, sir.

LARSEN:
It's just as well. You're mate just the same. When you're through with that job, you'll get your stuff and go aft.
(he turns to Leach, who is still standing there)
What are you standing around for?

LEACH:
I didn't sign for boat puller. I signed for cabin boy. I don't want no boat pullin'. It's a dirty—filthy heartbreakin' job—

LARSEN:
(smiling)
I thought you said you never sailed on a schooner before...

LEACH:
I once read about it in a book.

LARSEN:
(exploding)
Pack up and go for'ard...you filthy scum.

Leach stands there defiantly.

JOHNSON:
(moving towards him and placing his arm on his elbow)
Ye'd better do as he says, boy.

89. CLOSE SHOT   LEACH
as he throws off Johnson's arm.

LEACH:
(his eyes blazing defiance)
He's not talkin' to a dog, he's talkin' to a man.

90. MEDIUM CLOSE   TRUCKING SHOT

34   *The Sea Wolf*

as Larsen slowly walks off the bridge and comes towards Leach. There is an ominous pause.

91. MEDIUM CLOSE   LARSEN AND LEACH   OTHERS IN B.G.
Larsen comes close to Leach.

> **LARSEN:**
> *(his voice deadly)*
> So you're a man, Leach?
>
> **LEACH:**
> I've spit in the eye of better men than you for sayin' less.
>
> **LARSEN:**
> *(smiling at his insolence)*
> Ye're disobeyin' orders, Leach.
>
> **LEACH:**
> I don't like the way you give them.

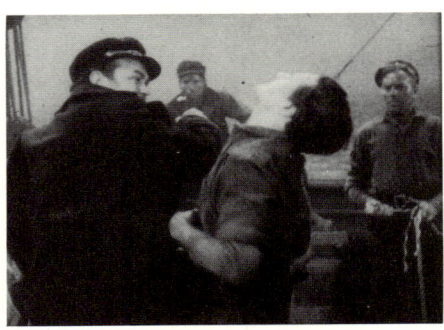

Suddenly Larsen springs. He buries his fist deep into Leach's stomach. As Leach doubles up in agony, he hits him twice in the face . . . short, powerful blows. As Leach hits the deck with terrific force, Larsen picks him up and hits him again. It is a brutal, horrible beating that does not cease until Leach slumps to the deck and lies there, like a limp, wet rag. Larsen looks down at him, then at Van Weyden.

> **LARSEN:**
> Do you still feel like refusing, Mr. Van Weyden?

(Van Weyden drops his eyes)
Get into the galley, Cooky'll show you what there is to do.

Van Weyden stands there looking at him. His whole expression is filled with revulsion at what he has just seen. Suddenly he makes a dash for the rail.

CAMERA SWINGS WITH HIM:

92. MEDIUM CLOSE   AT RAIL   SHOOTING TOWARDS SEA
In the distance can still be seen the fast disappearing sail of the pilot boat.

VAN WEYDEN:
(his voice filled with terror and desperation)
Ahoy! Pilot boat! Ahoy!! Pilot boat! Can you hear me...Pilot boat?[27]

93. MEDIUM GROUP SHOT   LARSEN AND THE MEN
A smile of derision comes over Larsen's face. He seems amused by Van Weyden's futile antics.

94. MEDIUM CLOSE   VAN WEYDEN   AT RAIL
as he stands there gripping the rail. He turns slowly and faces Larsen and the crew. Their laughter comes OVER the scene.

95. WIDER ANGLE[28]
as Larsen, again brisk and authoritative, turns to Svenson, who is about finished sewing up the neck.

LARSEN:
All right, Svenson...you finished with this job?
(Svenson nods)
Call all hands. We might as well have the funeral and get it over with.

Svenson gets up and pipes the hands.

96. FULL SHOT   THE BOAT
as the men stop their work and stream forward to gather

around the body. Two sailors lift the body up on a hatch and poise it over the sea.

CAMERA PANS TO:

97. THE FACES OF THE MEN
still, sullen, brooding, defiantly as they hastily pull off their caps. CAMERA HOLDS for an instant on Van Weyden, his eyes forward, his eyes lowered, and then COMES TO REST ON:

98. TIGHT TWO SHOT   WOLF LARSEN AND VAN WEYDEN
Van Weyden stares fascinated at the man. Up above the wind has increased and it makes a weird noise as it whistles through the sails. There is a moment of silence, broken only by the noise of the sea, the wind, and the ship.

> **LARSEN:**
> I only remember the last part of the service...that'll have to do.
> *(a pause as he tries to recollect, then he speaks slowly)*
> "And the body shall be cast into the sea..."
> *(brutally)*
> All right...what are you standing around for?...Cast it in.

The SOUND of the body striking the sea with a great splash is HEARD. The SOUND of the splash causes Van Weyden to wince involuntarily. Larsen looks at him and his lips curl into his usual contemptuous smile as we—

FADE OUT.

FADE IN

99. CLOSE SHOT   A PAIR OF HANDS
dirty, scarred with burns and scalds and with cracked, blackened fingernails, sloshing around in fat, congealed dish water, clumsily washing a greasy cooking pot.

CAMERA DRAWS BACK TO:

100. CLOSE SHOT   VAN WEYDEN
     as he stands in the galley cleaning up. His appearance has changed considerably, his clothes are torn . . . he is unshaven . . . on his face is a beard of several days' growth . . . his eyes are bloodshot. It is evident that he has gone through quite an ordeal.

>   **COOKY'S VOICE:**
>   *(o.s.)*
>   "from five in the morning till ten at night I am forced to listen..."

Van Weyden looks up, his eyes reflecting his anger.

101. MEDIUM CLOSE   COOKY
     as he sits on a stove in the kitchen, his feet resting on the stove. He is holding a sheaf of papers in his hand, from which he is reading. On his face is a diabolical grin. He is evidently enjoying himself immensely.

>   **COOKY:**
>   *(reading aloud)*
>   "...to 'is oily, insinuatin' tones, to watch 'is greasy smile an' to endure 'is..."
>   *(he hesitates making out the word)*
>   "monstrous self-conceit."
>   *(looks over at Van Weyden)*
>   Is that me you're writin' about?

102. WIDER ANGLE
     as Van Weyden moves towards him.

>   **VAN WEYDEN:**[29]
>   If you think the descriptions fit you...
>
>   **COOKY:**
>   *(sharply)*
>   Keep a civil tongue in your 'ead an' finish cleanin' up that slop.

Van Weyden resumes his work.

COOKY:
(shakes his head sadly)
Strike me blind if this ayn't gratitude for yu! 'Ere you come, a pore miserable specimin of 'uman scum, an' I tykes you into my galley an' treats you 'ansome...an' you write lies abaht me...I've a good mind to bash yer 'ead in with a fryin' pan...
(he picks up the paper as though to read again)

VAN WEYDEN:
(hotly)
You've no right to read that.

COOKY:
(ignoring him and continuing)
"But 'es but one portrait in a gallery of rogues"
(he nods his head in approval)
A well-turned phrase, I must s'y.
(he goes back to his reading)
"The men on board this ship, with the exception of a few, are all cast in the syme mold as their master. "Wolf" Larsen...a brutal, callous and inhuman lot"
(Cooky shakes his head sadly)
I'd hate to be in your shoes when Larsen reads this.

VAN WEYDEN:
You're not going to show it to him?

COOKY:
(superciliously)
H'its my duty as a loyal member of the crew,
(again he continues his reading)
"I keep thinking about the woman lying ill below deck..."
(Cooky grins at Van Weyden)
You an' me both, matey.
(he goes back to his reading)
"...and the tragic fate that seems to hang over her...that sends her from one evil to another..."

(Cooky wipes away a mock tear and begins to sniffle. Suddenly he looks up as a thought strikes him)
So you've met 'er before, 'ave ye?

103. REVERSE ANGLE   FAVORING VAN WEYDEN
As Van Weyden approaches Cooky.

> **VAN WEYDEN:**[30]
> *(slowly)*
> Are you going to give me those papers?
>
> **COOKY:**
> *(triumphantly)*
> Ye 'ave met 'er, haven't ye?
>
> **VAN WEYDEN:**
> Whether I have or not is not your concern. Give me those papers.
>
> **COOKY:**
> *(insolently)*
> I tole you...it's my duty to turn 'em over to the proper authorities.
>
> **VAN WEYDEN:**
> You're not only a common thief...but an informer as well.

There is a pause. Cooky slowly rises from his stove and faces Van Weyden.

> **COOKY:**
> *(viciously)*
> Informer and thief, is it?
>
> **VAN WEYDEN:**
> I had a purse in the clothes that you so *graciously* changed for me...That purse is now empty...no one else but you...
>
> **COOKY:**
> *(grabbing him by the collar)*
> Ye'll keep yer mouth shut, d'ye 'ear?

104. TIGHT TWO SHOT   VAN WEYDEN AND COOKY
as the two men stand facing each other.

> **VAN WEYDEN:**
> If I get those notes back...
>
> **COOKY:**
> The only thing ye'll get from me is the back of me 'and.

Suiting the action to the words, he slaps Van Weyden[31] in the mouth with the back of his hand, sending him staggering against the stove.

105. WIDER ANGLE
as Van Weyden hits the stove. Suddenly he lifts the stove handle and swinging it, is about to go for Cooky. From nowhere, a knife appears in Cooky's hand. There is a tense pause.

> **COOKY:**
> *(malevolently)*
> Once in Liverpool 'Is Worship gave me two years for knifin' a man...on board this ship it's not a criminal offense.

Suddenly o.s. is HEARD six bells. They both stop and listen.

> **COOKY:**
> Six bells. The men will be eating soon.
> *(sharply)*
> Now get back to your work.

Van Weyden slowly puts the handle down and resumes his work. Cooky grins and then resumes his seat and picks up the papers.

> **COOKY:**[32]
> *(grinning)*
> It's a very pleasurable feelin' to be givin' orders for a chynge instead of tykin' 'em...

(he leans back contentedly)
I'm enjoyin' it no end,

DISSOLVE TO:

106. CLOSE SHOT   A SHIP'S LAMP
as it swings violently from the ceiling beam to which[33] it is attached, giving us the feeling of the violent motion of the boat. O.S. is HEARD the chimes of the ship's bell. They toll eight times.

CAMERA DRAWS BACK AND PANS DOWN TO:

107. MEDIUM SHOT   INTERIOR OF OFFICERS' MESS
About six men are seated at the table, eating. Larsen sits at the head of it . . . on one side of him is Svenson, the new mate, on the other LOUIE, the ship's doctor. Everything about him seems bloated . . . his body, his hands, his lips and his eyes, which are almost always three quarters closed. In front of him is a bottle of liquor from which he constantly keeps drinking. The others are all cut from pretty much the same stripe, taciturn, cold-eyed and ruthless-looking men. Overhead the swinging lamp casts crazy patterns of light and shadow over the faces of the men, giving to the scene a grotesque quality. Van Weyden enters scene, carrying a tray of dishes.

108. MEDIUM CLOSE   AT HEAD OF TABLE
as Van Weyden approaches Larsen. It is evident that he is having a very difficult time maintaining his balance against the violent pitching of the boat.[34] As he performs the precarious job of setting the plates down, the men watch him, an amused smile on their lips. He manages to lay the last one, which is Svenson's and then loses his balance, spilling the contents of the plate over Svenson and falling backwards. A roar of laughter goes up, but Svenson doesn't think it funny. He gets up and raising his heavy hob-nailed boot, kicks Van Weyden in the small of the back . . . then sits down again at his place.

LARSEN:
(turns to Van Weyden lying on the floor)
All right...get up. You haven't finished your work.

109. CLOSE SHOT   VAN WEYDEN
as he struggles to his feet. Almost bent over double with pain, he approaches the table again.

110. MEDIUM CLOSE   AT TABLE
as Van Weyden approaches. Larsen looks at him, then turns away and talks to Svenson.

> **LARSEN:**
> *(to Svenson)*
> You like being mate, eh? It gives you a good feeling to be able to kick a man, doesn't it?
>
> **SVENSON:**
> *(pride in his voice)*
> A couple of hours ago I beat Johnson up.
>
> **LARSEN:**
> *(angrily)*
> I need my crew to work this ship. I can't afford to have them lying battered up below decks.
>
> **SVENSON:**[35]
> *(apologetically)*
> I didn't hurt him too bad...he's still at work. You told me to maintain discipline, didn't you? He was...
> (he thinks for a moment)
> He was inciting a mutiny.
>
> **LARSEN:**
> *(quietly)*
> What did he say?
>
> **SVENSON:**
> He asked too many questions.
>
> **LARSEN:**
> *(quickly)*
> Does he know anything about my brother's ship...the "Macedonia"?[36]
>
> **SVENSON:**
> I don't think so, sir.

LARSEN:
(turning to the men)
None of you have been talking, have you?

There is a pause. The men shake their heads in denial.

LARSEN:
None of you better. So far as the crew is concerned we're hunting seals and the longer they think so...the better for all of us.

SMOKE:
I'm not so sure of that, sir. If your brother's ship ever catches up to us...we may need 'em to fight for us.

LARSEN:
They'll fight...or drown.

Suddenly he puts his hand to his head as though he had been struck by a blow on the head. He buries his head in his hands. There is a pause as the men look at him and then at each other.

SMOKE:
(shaking Louie)
Hey, Louie...do somethin' the Captain's got another one of his headaches...

LARSEN:
(quickly—a slight trace of fear in his voice)
No...no...it's nothing...it's gone away...[37] it's all right. You don't have to do anything. It's all right
(the struggle against the pain is reflected on his face)

110a. CLOSE SHOT   VAN WEYDEN
as he reacts to this.

110b. MEDIUM CLOSE   AT TABLE
as Larsen finally regains control. He turns to Svenson.

LARSEN:
What questions did Johnson ask?

SVENSON:
He wanted to know why we keep changing our course all the time...why we have a cannon on board a sailing schooner.

LARSEN:
Did you answer him?

SVENSON:
With a marlin spike on the side of the head.
(quickly)
But not too hard.

The men all laugh. Suddenly Louie arises. From his condition and his closed eyes, it is obvious that he has had too much. He turns to Svenson.

LOUIE:
Did I hear you say that you hit somebody with a marlin spike?
(Svenson nods)
I'll go and put some stitches in his head.

Larsen pulls Louie down into his chair.

LARSEN:
Sit down, Louie, and finish drinking your supper. In the condition you're in, now, you're liable to put your stitches in the wrong place.

The men laugh as Louie, shrugging his shoulders, listlessly sits down. An amused glint comes into Larsen's eyes. He looks at Van Weyden, then speaks pointedly to Louie.

LARSEN:
How's your patient, Louie?

LOUIE:
(in act of taking drink)[38]
Huh?
(he puts bottle down)

Oh...my patient...she's all right...I guess.
(he takes another drink)

LARSEN:
(pointedly)
You'll take good care of her, Louie? She's a friend of our literary cabin boy.

111. CLOSE SHOT   VAN WEYDEN
    as he reacts to this.

112. MEDIUM CLOSE   LARSEN AND LOUIE   VAN WEYDEN IN BACKGROUND.
    Larsen notices Van Weyden's reaction. He smiles faintly.

LARSEN:
(he is evidently taunting Van Weyden)
A tragic fate hangs over her, Louie.

LOUIE:
(he is a little drunk by now)
It's possible.

LARSEN:
With you taking care of her, it's more than possible.
(he turns to Van Weyden)
Louie has a perfect record on board this ship. He's never cured a patient yet.

LOUIE:
(suddenly)
It's not my fault...the men are half dead by the time they get to me. I'm a good doctor.

ONE OF THE MEN:
(shouting up to him)
Doctor! You're a faker!

LOUIE:
(rising to his feet)
That's a lie...it's a dirty lie...I graduated from three universities...I was the head of a clinic...I've per-

formed great operations...I could perform them again...if I had the instruments and...
(suddenly he stops and looks down at his hands. He speaks pitifully like a small boy)
...my hands didn't shake...so much.
(he looks up at Van Weyden)
It's a funny thing...but...but I can't control my hands ...anymore.
(suddenly, desperately to Van Weyden)
You...you're a stranger...you look like an intelligent man...you believe me, don't you?

VAN WEYDEN:
Sure, sure...I believe you.

LOUIE:
(triumphantly)
See...see...*he* believes me...*Somebody* believes me.
(suddenly he stops and draws himself up proudly)
I've...I've...got to get back to my patient.

113. WIDER ANGLE
    as Louie goes out, a ludicrous, staggering drunken figure. A burst of laughter goes up as the door slams behind him. Van Weyden, taking advantage of the laughter, slips out of the room into a door leading to Larsen's cabin. Larsen notices this ... smiles ... and then resumes his eating. O.S. comes the SOUND of the men's laughter.

114. MEDIUM CLOSE   LARSEN'S CABIN
    as Van Weyden enters. The room is in complete darkness.[39] Van Weyden strikes a match, and lights a lamp throwing the room into bold relief. Putting the lamp down, he goes over to Larsen's bunk and begins to straighten it out. He looks about the room. The first thing that strikes his attention is a map on the wall.

115. INSERT: MAP
    It is a chart of the Pacific Ocean ... including the Japanese Islands. The CAMERA MOVES with Van Weyden's gaze along the wall and then suddenly comes to rest on a bookshelf.

116. CLOSE SHOT   THE BOOKSHELF
On it, neatly held together by two bookends, is a row of books. THE CAMERA PANS ALONG the shelf, picking out such names as Shakespeare, Tennyson, Poe and De Quincey, intermingled with scientific works like Tyndel, Proctor, Darwin and Nietzsche.

117. MEDIUM CLOSE   AT BUNK
Van Weyden stares as though he can't believe his eyes, then his eyes drop to an opened book that lies on the blanket. He picks it up and glances at it.

118. INSERT: THE BOOK
It is a copy of Milton's "Paradise Lost." A section of the page is marked off . . .

> Here at least,
> We shall be free;
> Here we may reign secure, and,
> in my choice
> To reign is worth ambition,
> though in hell,
> *Better to reign in Hell than*
> *serve in Heaven.*[40]

The last two lines are underlined. Suddenly a swath of light illumines Van Weyden's face. He looks up quickly.

119. MEDIUM CLOSE   AT DOOR WOLF LARSEN
as he stands there, a smile playing on his lips.

120. REVERSE ANGLE   FAVORING VAN WEYDEN
as Larsen approaches him. He gets up.

> **VAN WEYDEN:**
> *(nervously)*
> Cooky told me to clean up in here. I thought I'd get through before the men finished eating. I happened to find this book open...and...
>
> **LARSEN:**[41]
> Sit down, Van Weyden.

(Van Weyden sits down. Larsen pulls up a chair next to him. He points to the book in his hand)
That's a great poem, isn't it?
(Van Weyden is silent)
Talk up, man!!

VAN WEYDEN:
(automatically)
Yes, it's a great poem.

LARSEN:
Milton really understood the devil, didn't he?
(he reads aloud the last two lines)
"Better to reign in Hell than serve in Heaven."
(he shakes his head in admiration)
That's a great line.

Van Weyden stares at him as though fascinated . . . Then his eyes wander to the row of books on the shelf. Larsen, an amused look in his eyes, follows his gaze.

LARSEN:
This is the first time you've ever been in my cabin, isn't it?
(Van Weyden nods)
You didn't expect to find anything like this, did you?
(he nods towards the books, laughing)
I really read them, too.
(suddenly his voice grows harsh)

Maybe it would have been better if I'd never opened a book...
(a pause. The laughter comes back into his eyes)
Cooky gave me your notes. I read them.
(Van Weyden starts up involuntarily)
You don't have to be afraid. I enjoyed them. You write very well.

VAN WEYDEN:
(there is a trace of sarcasm in his voice)
Thank you...

LARSEN:
(quoting from his notes)
"A brutal, calloused and inhuman lot...cast in the same mold as their master..."
(he laughs)
I wonder what you'll be like, Van Weyden, when this voyage is over...

VAN WEYDEN:
You think I'll change.

LARSEN:
Oh yes...very much.

VAN WEYDEN:
I don't think so, Larsen.

Larsen suddenly reaches out and hits him in the stomach, doubling him up.

LARSEN:
(laughing)
That's part of your education, Van Weyden...You must say...*Captain* Larsen or *sir*. Remember there's a difference in our social standing on board this vessel.
(he looks at Van Weyden still struggling to catch his breath)
What class of society do you belong to on land, Van Weyden?
(Van Weyden is silent)

LARSEN:
You needn't answer. It's written all over you.
(cynically)
A good education, breeding, refinement, sensitivity ...you've got all the things that money can buy... including money.

VAN WEYDEN:
Whatever money I have, I've earned from my books.

LARSEN:
You actually earn money?[42]

VAN WEYDEN:
Ten thousand a year.

LARSEN:
(whistling)[43]
That's quite a lot. You must be pretty good. What kind of books do you write?

VAN WEYDEN:
All sorts of fiction...

LARSEN:
Fiction? Nothing important?

There is a pause.

VAN WEYDEN:
No nothing very important.

LARSEN:
(suddenly)
But you don't have to make all that money.[44] If something were to happen to you...like losing your arms or your legs...
(a strange bitter note comes into his voice)
Or going blind...
(he resumes his former bantering note)
Someone would take care of you...your family...your friends...they wouldn't be a brutal, calloused and inhuman lot, would they?

> *(suddenly his tone changes. It becomes angry)*
> You wouldn't have to struggle for bread...you wouldn't have to live in a world where your hand was turned against every man's, and every man's against yours...
> *(bitterly)*
> Even your own brother's...
>
> **VAN WEYDEN:**
> *(suddenly—a note of mockery in his voice)*
> You seem to find it quite necessary to justify yourself to me, don't you, *Captain* Larsen?

There is a pause. Larsen's face goes livid with rage, then he controls himself. He laughs.

> **LARSEN:**
> My strength justifies me, *Mr.* Van Weyden. The fact that I can kill you, or let you live as I choose...the fact that I control the destinies of all on board this ship...
> *(his voice rises again)*
> The fact that it's my will...and my will alone that rules here...that's justification enough.

There is a pause. Van Weyden turns to go.

121. WIDER ANGLE
as Van Weyden starts to go toward the door.

> **LARSEN:**
> Where're you going?
>
> **VAN WEYDEN:**
> Cooky's expecting me in the galley.
>
> **LARSEN:**
> *(a lonely note in his voice)*
> Don't go...let him wait. It's a long time since I've talked like this...to anyone.

Van Weyden steps and stands with his back braced against the door.

52 The Sea Wolf

122. MEDIUM CLOSE SHOT
as Larsen walks over to him.

> LARSEN:
> What do you intend doing with those notes of yours?
>
> VAN WEYDEN:
> *(shrugging his shoulders)*
> Perhaps some day I'll write a book about my voyage on the "Ghost."
>
> LARSEN:
> *(with a touch of vanity, eagerly)*
> You'll write about me too in this book, won't you?
>
> VAN WEYDEN:
> You'll be the leading character.
>
> LARSEN:
> *(as he speaks, there is a sort of mad gleam in his eyes which one associates only with a psychopathic ego-maniac)*
> That's a good idea...a book about me. I'll help you with it...we'll spend lots of time together. I'll tell you stories about my early life...stories that'll make them understand—
> *(suddenly he stops himself, realizing he has let himself go too far; almost snarling at this display of weakness on his part)*
> What difference does it make to me whether anybody understands or not?

There is a pause. Larsen stands there thinking for a moment. The same mad gleam comes back into his eyes. He seems to be delving into his past.

> LARSEN:
> Ah yes...I could tell you many things...of the bleak coast town where I was born...of my mother and father...peasants of the sea, who sowed their sons upon the waves and got in return nothing but hunger and misery. Five brothers I had...four of them are dead... drowned like rats, in the foc'sles of leakin', rotten

ships...That's not for me. I'll choose my death, like I've chosen my life.

He begins to pace up and down, speaking like a man possessed. CAMERA TRUCKS with him.

123. CLOSE TRUCKING SHOT   LARSEN

> **LARSEN:**
> Cabin boy at 12...ship's boy at 14...ordinary seaman at 16...Master and owner of my own vessel at 21! All by myself I did it!! I learned everything by myself... navigation, mathematics, science, literature...

124. WIDER ANGLE
as Larsen suddenly stops and grabs Van Weyden by the collar. His face is white with his intensity.

> **LARSEN:**
> All of this...all of this I want written down. Do you hear me?...all of this...

Suddenly, o.s., is heard a knock on the door. Larsen releases Van Weyden. They both turn.[45]

> **LARSEN:**
> Yes?...

125. MEDIUM CLOSE   DOOR
as the door opens and Leach enters. He stands there silhoutted against the light from the other room. It is quite apparent that the hatred he feels for Larsen has not diminished. Instead it has grown. It is evident in his eyes and in his talk. The way he speaks to Larsen makes you feel that it is an effort for him to restrain himself.

> **LEACH:**
> The First Mate wants you to come down below deck, sir.

126. WIDER ANGLE
as Larsen approaches him.

> LARSEN:
> What's wrong?
>
> LEACH:
> The woman, sir. I think she's dying.
>
> LARSEN:
> What are you bothering me for? Let Louie take care of it. He's the doctor on board this ship.
>
> LEACH:
> Louie's in no condition to take care of anything, sir. He's too drunk.
>
> LARSEN:
> *(there is a pause, viciously)*
> All right.
> *(he starts to go; looks at Van Weyden)*
> You can come along too. This might give you something else to write in that book of yours.

He exits as Van Weyden looks at him, then at Leach and follows him out as we

DISSOLVE TO:

127. CLOSE SHOT   RUTH   INTERIOR SICK BAY
as she lies in bed, her face white, her lips closed, her breath coming in irregular rhythms.

CAMERA DRAWS BACK TO:

128. MEDIUM CLOSE   AT BEDSIDE   COOKY
He sits next to her, holding one of her hands in his. He keeps methodically stroking her hand gently, as though he were afraid of injuring it. In his eyes there is a strange mixture of fright and desire.

> LARSEN'S VOICE:
> Cooky!

He drops her hand and turns toward the door. His eyes are filled with terror.

129. WIDER ANGLE
as Larsen, Van Weyden and Leach enter.

> **COOKY:**
> *(his voice tense, his fear evident)*
> I was tryin' to see if there was any life left in her. I was 'oldin' 'er pulse, sir.
> *(he gets up cringing as though expecting a blow)*
>
> **LARSEN:**
> What are you doing in here?
>
> **COOKY:**
> The myte arsked me to stay with 'er, sir, until you arrived....that's the truth, sir, you can arsk 'im, sir.
> *(he looks at Ruth, then suddenly blurts out)*
> She's orful purty...it's a bloody shyme she 'as to die...
>
> **LARSEN:**
> Shut up!...

His gaze wanders about the room.

CAMERA PANS TO:

130. MEDIUM CLOSE   LOUIE
He sits slumped in a chair, his head resting on his chest, his arms dangling from his sides, his eyes closed. On the floor below him is an empty bottle. The motion of the ship keeps jerking him to and fro, like a marionette.

> **LARSEN'S VOICE:**
> *(o.s.)*
> Did you try to wake him up?
>
> **COOKY'S VOICE:**
> *(o.s.)*
> 'Taint much use, sir...when Louie gets 'is snootful like this 'e's out for at least a whole d'y.

131. MEDIUM CLOSE   AT BEDSIDE

>   **LARSEN:**
>   *(turns to Leach)*
>   Leach...see if you can bring that drunken swine to.

Leach goes over to Louie and begins to try to revive him.

>   **VAN WEYDEN:**
>   *(who has knelt down beside Ruth)*
>   She's breathing rather hard, as though she were choking.
>
>   **LARSEN:**
>   Open that porthole, Cooky.
>
>   **COOKY:**
>   We're in an 'eavy sea, sir, we'll be drenched.
>
>   **LARSEN:**
>   *(cutting him short)*
>   Open it!!

Cooky goes to the porthole and opens it. As he does so,[46] a burst of spray from the ocean blows into the room and extinguishes the light. Cooky quickly strikes a match and relights the lamp, handing it to Larsen. CAMERA TRUCKS with Larsen as, holding the lamp high, he goes over to Louie and Leach.

132. MEDIUM CLOSE   LOUIE   OTHERS IN B.G.
Louie still lies in his drunken stupor.

>   **LARSEN:**
>   *(to Leach)*
>   Well?
>
>   **LEACH:**
>   I can't seem to do much with him, sir. Every time I get him awake, he keeps dropping off again.

Suddenly Larsen lifts Louie, halfway up from his chair, and begins to slap him, first with the palm, then with the back of his hand. Louie begins to moan.

LOUIE:
(intuitively trying to shield himself, muttering drunkenly)
No...no...don't...don't hit me...don't hit me...

LARSEN:[47]
(viciously)
Keep awake...you drunken...

LOUIE:
(groaning)
Don't hit me...don't hit me.

LEACH:
(quickly)
He's awake now, sir.

LARSEN:
Make sure he stays awake.

COOKY:
I've got some 'ot coffee boiling on the stove. I'll go get it.

LARSEN:
No, you stay here—I'll probably need you.
(he looks up at Leach)
Leach! Go down to the galley. Bring back that pot of coffee and be quick about it.

Leach gets up and leaves.

133. TIGHT TWO SHOT   AT BEDSIDE   RUTH AND VAN WEYDEN
Van Weyden bends close to her as her lips begin to form words.

RUTH:
(her breath coming in short gasps)
Two men...they're coming in here...
(her eyes open. There is terror in them)
They'll ask questions...you'll say you know me.

VAN WEYDEN:[48]
Yes...yes...I'll say it...I'll say it.

58   *The Sea Wolf*

She lapses into unconsciousness again.

134. WIDER ANGLE
as Larsen comes into scene. Cooky hovers in the b.g. O.S. comes the SOUND of Louie's moaning. Van Weyden looks up at Larsen.

> **LARSEN:**
> What was she saying?

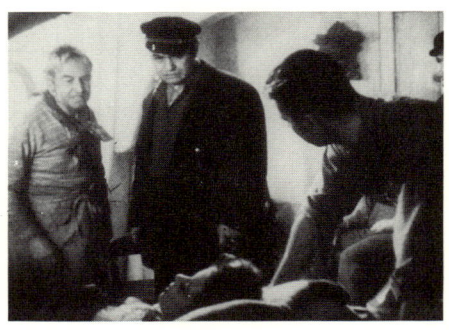

> **VAN WEYDEN:**
> *(quickly)*
> I couldn't make it out.
>
> **COOKY:**
> 'E's lyin', sir...'E could...'e did. I 'eard 'im answer 'er back.

Suddenly the girl begins to mutter again. They bend low to catch her whispered phrases.

135. TIGHT GROUP SHOT   AT BED
as they listen.

> **RUTH:**
> I won't let them take me back...You don't know what being in prison is like...I'd rather die...I'd rather die...
> *(her voice trails off again)*

There is a pause.

> COOKY:
> Well strike me pink!...a convict...a bloody, snivelin',
> snarlin', no good con...
> *(his face lights up in pleasure)*
> She's not a lydey...she's one of us...

Larsen looks at him, then starts to laugh as though his sides would break.

> COOKY:
> *(bewildered)*
> 'Ave I said somethin' that strikes you funny, sir?...

Larsen continues to laugh.

> COOKY:
> *(fawning at him)*
> I'm pleased, sir...I'm arful pleased...

> LARSEN:
> *(to Van Weyden)*
> You don't appreciate the humor of this, Van Weyden. Here this boat is already loaded to the gunwales with as varied an assortment of derelicts and outcasts as ever sailed before the same mast...and what do we fish up out of the sea? As Cooky puts it, "another one" of us.[49]
> *(there is a trace of bitterness in his voice)*
> There must be a magnetic attraction about this ship...something that draws these dregs of the earth to it...like slimy barnacles clinging to its keel...
> *(suddenly he stops, looks at Van Weyden strangely)*
> Or maybe it's me...maybe I attract them.
> *(his laughter fills the room again)*

O.S. is HEARD the sound of the door opening.

136. WIDER ANGLE
as Leach enters, carrying the steaming pot of coffee. He goes directly over to Louie and begins to force it down his throat.

60 The Sea Wolf

Louie sputters and spats as the hot liquid burns his tongue. Wildly, he tries to push the coffee cup out of Leach's hand.

137. MEDIUM GROUP SHOT   FAVORING LOUIE AND LEACH   OTHERS IN B.G.
as Leach keeps trying to force the coffee down, Louie's senses return to him. He shakes his head, rubs his eyes and notices Leach for the first time.

> **LOUIE:**
> *(his tongue still thick, his eyes still slightly glazed)*
> I had a dream...a horrible dream...[50] someone kept hitting me...I begged them to stop, but they wouldn't... they kept on hitting me...
> *(suddenly his eyes stop roaming. They focus on the face of Larsen.)*
> It wasn't a dream.

Larsen moves closer to him. Into Louie's eyes comes a look of terror. He speaks quickly.

> **LOUIE:**
> What else could I do but sit here and get drunk?
> *(he waves in the direction of Ruth)*
> I can't save her...she's as good as gone.
> *(he reaches for the bottle)*
> I need another drink.[51]

Van Weyden quickly pulls the bottle away from him.

> **VAN WEYDEN:**
> Listen to me...

> **LARSEN:**
> *(a cruel smile on his lips)*
> Let him have his drink...he's no good for anything else.

> **VAN WEYDEN:**
> We can't just let her die like this...there must be some last, forlorn[52] chance...

LOUIE:
Sure...sure...there is...
(grandly)
I could perform a blood transfusion.

VAN WEYDEN:
(turning on him fiercely)
Well...?

LOUIE:
(laughing bitterly)
On board this ship...with the instruments I have...that's like asking me to perform a miracle...

VAN WEYDEN:
(explosively)
All right...then perform one!

LOUIE:
(evasively)
I can't...I need...[53]

LARSEN:
(sneering)
What he needs he'll never find again...he's lost his nerve. Am I right, Louie?

There is a pause.

138. TIGHT GROUP SHOT   LEACH, VAN WEYDEN AND LOUIE
Louie sits there, looking first at Larsen, then at Leach, then suddenly he buries his head in his hands. Both Van Weyden and Leach look at each other across his bowed head. There is a smile of triumph on Larsen's face. Suddenly Van Weyden kneels down beside Louie.

VAN WEYDEN:
Louie...listen to me...you asked me before if I believed in you...I said I did.

LOUIE:
No...no...it might happen again...I couldn't stand it if it did. I'd kill myself. This way her life is not in my

hands. It's in the hands of fate. I've got nothing to do with it.

LARSEN:
(cynically to Van Weyden)[54]
There's your human soul rising to immortal heights... unselfish, noble...

LOUIE:
(to Van Weyden, desperately trying to justify himself)
You can't just perform a blood transfusion...you've got to be sure that the blood is alike...

LARSEN:
(an amused gleam in his eye)
Don't let that stop you, Louie...
(he turns out of shot)
Leach!!

139. WIDER ANGLE
as Leach approaches Larsen.

LEACH:
Yes, sir?

LARSEN:
You'll give your blood for this woman, won't you?

LEACH:
(without hesitation)
Certainly, sir.

LARSEN:
(turning to Louie)
Well, go ahead, Louie...you're lucky...
(smiling)
I'll guarantee that their blood is alike.[55]

There is a pause. Louie looks at him a bit puzzled. Van Weyden's face goes white as he realizes the implication of the remark. Suddenly Cooky lets out a loud guffaw.

COOKY:
I get the point...don't ye get it, Louie? They've both

got the syme kind of blood. She's a con...'e's a con...got it? That's what the cap'n means...jailbird's blood. Funny, ain't it?[56]

Leach's eyes blaze with anger. He springs at Cooky's throat. Before they can be stopped, they are both rolling on the floor. Larsen springs in and tries to pull Leach off him. As he succeeds in doing so, Cooky whips the knife from his pocket and slashes viciously at Leach. As Leach throws up his arm to protect his face, the knife rips his forearm open, sending the blood spurting.

140. MEDIUM CLOSE   LEACH AND LARSEN   OTHERS IN BACKGROUND
as Leach stands there, looking down at his gashed forearm, trying to stop the flow of blood.

> **LARSEN:**
> *(he turns to Louie, goading him)*
> Well, Louie...go on. Let's see you do it. You've even got yourself an assistant. Cooky's done the first part of the job for you. You'd better get that blood quickly before it cools off.

Leach, still holding onto his arm, looks at Larsen. He is trying hard to control his anger. CAMERA PANS his gaze around the room, INCLUDING Van Weyden, Louie, the terrified Cooky and finally COMES TO REST on the girl.

141. CLOSE SHOT   HER ARM
hanging limply from the bed.

                                  CAMERA SWINGS BACK SHARPLY TO:

142. CLOSE SHOT   LEACH'S ARM
as his other hand still clutches it tightly in an effort to stem the flow of blood.

                                      CAMERA DRAWS BACK TO:

143. FULL SHOT   LEACH
Suddenly the expression on his face changes completely. His

clenched jaws relax and a sinister grin spreads over his face. They all look at him, a bit puzzled by his change of attitude.

> **LEACH:**
> *(grinning as though a peculiar idea which is his alone has struck him; slowly)*
> You don't have to worry, Captain. This kind of blood never cools off.

He stands there grinning defiantly and mysteriously at Larsen, as the doctor, looking at Van Weyden's pleading face, impulsively bends down to begin the transfusion.[57]

FADE OUT.

FADE IN

144. LONG SHOT THE "GHOST" DAY
sailing along in a rather heavy sea.

DISSOLVE THRU TO:

145. MEDIUM SHOT THE DECK
The crew is busy at work. In the b.g. the group of hunters lies sprawled on some ropes, playing cards.

146. MEDIUM CLOSE TRUCKING SHOT
as Larsen walks along the deck making the rounds. As he passes the men, each of one looks at him sullenly, hatefully. But he seems to have no eyes for them. Suddenly he passes a young boy, a sailor who is standing up against the rail, his face white, his head in his hands.[58] Larsen stops.

147. MEDIUM CLOSE LARSEN AND BOY
as Larsen looks down at the boy.

> **LARSEN:**
> *(his voice cruel)*
> Resting...?

>BOY:
>I don't feel well, sir.
>
>LARSEN:
>*(viciously)*
>Maybe this'll make you feel better.

He lifts the boy up and shoves him forward. The boy stumbles a few steps under the impetus of the shove, then pitches forward to the deck.

148. MEDIUM GROUP SHOT
    as the sailors suddenly stop work. Leach springs forward and tries to help the boy up to his feet.

    >LARSEN:
    >Leave him be! Get to work!
    >
    >LEACH:
    >The kid is really sick, sir.
    >
    >LARSEN:
    >*(turning to the boy)*
    >Get forward!!

149. to 151.   OMITTED

152. WIDER ANGLE

    >LEACH:
    >Go down below, kid.
    >*(to Larsen)*
    >I'll do his work for him.
    >
    >LARSEN:
    >I said he was to go for'ard.
    >
    >LEACH:
    >What difference does it make to you as long as the work gets done...?
    >
    >LARSEN:
    >Leach...ever since you've come aboard this boat I've

had to beat you to a pulp at least once a day. Don't you ever get tired of it?

Harrison, a large burly sailor, moves forward.

HARRISON:
Maybe some time you won't have to beat just him alone.

There is a pause. Larsen looks around at the group. It is evident they are primed for trouble. Larsen smiles that deadly smile of his.

CUT TO:

153. THE HUNTERS
They have risen to their feet, stand there looking at the sailors surrounding Larsen. Suddenly one of them raises a rifle to his shoulder, fires quickly in the air.

CUT TO:

154. THE SKY   A SEAGULL
The wings of a sea gull that has been following the ship flutter suddenly, beat desperately in an effort to keep itself in the sky, and then the bird suddenly plunges into the sea.

155. MEDIUM GROUP SHOT   THE SAILORS AND LARSEN
The significance of the action is not lost on them. There is a pause. For a few seconds that seem almost like an eternity, a deathly silence hangs over the ship. Suddenly it is broken by the loud hysterical cackling of Cooky's laughter.

CUT TO:

156. MEDIUM SHOT   COOKY
as he stands framed in the hatchway, doubled up with laughter. He keeps pointing his finger at the steps below.

CAMERA SWINGS QUICKLY TO:

157. GROUP SHOT
as all heads turn in amazement at the strange antics of Cooky.

CUT TO:

158. CLOSE SHOT   THE HATCHWAY
as Louie emerges. His appearance is indeed cause for Cooky's hysterical laughter. He is no longer the same Louie. Somewhere, out of a chest perhaps, he has dug up an old moth-eaten cutaway suit. He wears a wing collar, a stiff shirt, the cuffs of which are ragged and frayed. He has trimmed his beard but that it is a home-made job is quite evident, for it is still uneven and scraggly. On his nose is perched a pair of pince-nez glasses. He draws himself up to as much height as he can possibly muster, looks at Cooky indignantly.

> LOUIE:
> Stop laughing, you idiot! Haven't you ever seen a man dressed up before?

Cooky's laughter suddenly trails down and dies away as out of the shadows of the hatchway appears the girl.

159. WIDER ANGLE
as Ruth appears. Her face is wan and tired, a fact which is accented by the heavy coating of makeup that she wears to cover it. She wears the same clothes she wore on the ferryboat, except one can see that her sojourn in the water has shrunk them a bit. The costume consists of a tight skirt, a blouse and a short pea jacket. Louie turns to her gallantly.

> LOUIE:
> Careful of the step, my dear...

He helps her up. As she crosses over the step, she looks about her. Despite her appearance of outward bravado, it is quite evident she is terribly frightened by this, her first appearance on deck. Louie notices this and smiles quickly.

> LOUIE
> *(extending his arm like a gallant old gentleman)*
> Your arm, my dear...

She puts her arm in his outstretched elbow. Together this pathetic pair walk down the deck toward Larsen and the men.

CUT TO:

160. CLOSE SHOT   VAN WEYDEN
as he notices the scene. He starts down the bridge.

161. REVERSE ANGLE   MEDIUM CLOSE   LARSEN   GROUP IN B.G.
as they approach . . . Louie in his new-found dignity, Ruth bravely trying to brazen out the situation. A glint of amusement comes into Larsen's eyes as he watches this. A smile spreads across his face.

> **LARSEN:**
> *(aside to the men out of the corner of his mouth)*
> I'll break the head of the first man who even so much as cracks a smile.

He turns and faces them. It is evident he intends to make the most of this situation.

162. WIDER ANGLE
as Louie and Ruth approach.

> **LOUIE:**
> *(speaking gingerly, with a professional air)*
> Captain Larsen...Miss Webster...

> *(he pronounces the words proudly)*
> My patient!

They nod acknowledgment to each other. Louie proudly points to her as though she were an inanimate object.

> **LOUIE:**
> She looks well for the first time on deck, doesn't she?[59] Color in her cheeks...
> *(he pinches them a bit)*
> Her eyes bright...her pulse normal...
> *(he laughs as though embarrassed)*
> I was telling Miss Webster how fortunate she was that she had a doctor of my professional standing attending her. The ordinary ship's doctor...
> *(he shrugs his shoulder deprecatingly)*
> Who knows what might have happened?

Larsen has all he can do to keep from laughing in his face.

> **LARSEN:**
> I'm glad to see that you're up and about, ma'am.

> **RUTH:**
> *(grandly)*
> Thank you for everything. I must have caused you a great deal of inconvenience.

> **LARSEN:**
> On the contrary, ma'am...I did nothing more than my Christian duty.

One of the hunters turns and hides his face to keep from laughing.

> **RUTH:**
> *(as she turns to Louie)*[60]
> The sailor who gave his blood...?

> **LOUIE:**
> Oh yes...yes...

> *(he motions to Leach)*
> Young man!
>
> **LEACH:**
> The name is Leach.
>
> **LOUIE:**
> I have a bad memory for names
> *(to Ruth)*
> This is he.
>
> **RUTH:**
> *(quickly)*
> I'm very grateful...young man.

There is a pause. Leach looks at her. There is scorn in his eyes. She notices it and avoids his glance.

> **RUTH:**
> *(quickly)*
> When I reach shore I'll see that you're well rewarded.

Leach is silent.

> **LARSEN:**
> *(to Leach)*
> Say "thank you" to the lady.
>
> **LEACH:**
> *(slowly)*
> Thank you, *lady*.

Ruth turns away from him. She is troubled by his constant stare. She looks about her as though seeking desperately for some reassurance. Suddenly her face brightens.

163. MEDIUM CLOSE   VAN WEYDEN
He has come down from the bridge and edged his way into the circle surrounding Larsen and Ruth. As her gaze meets his, he shakes his head slightly as though trying to warn her of something.

164. CLOSE SHOT   RUTH
    as she meets his eyes. She seems puzzled by his look. Into her eyes comes a questioning one as though she wanted him to re-assure her silently that nothing had gone wrong.

165. CLOSE SHOT   VAN WEYDEN
    as he drops his eyes trying to avoid answering the question in her eyes. He stops back and disappears behind the line of men.

166. CLOSE SHOT   LARSEN
    as he stands there watching this exchange of looks. He is becoming more and more amused.

167. MEDIUM GROUP SHOT
    as Larsen turns to Ruth.

> **LARSEN:**
> I'm sorry that I couldn't turn back and put you ashore when you were first picked up...but you were so sick I thought it was dangerous to move you.
>
> **LOUIE:**
> *(quickly)*
> That was *my* diagnosis.
>
> **LARSEN:**
> *(in mock humility)*
> I beg your pardon, *doctor*.

(he turns to Ruth)
The people you left behind...

RUTH:
(a worried look comes over her face)
People?...what people?

LARSEN:
(smiling at her apparent concern)
I mean your family...
(she looks relieved)
They've probably given you up for dead by now. I can imagine how glad they'll be to see you again when you land in 'Frisco again.

RUTH:
'Frisco...? You're going back to 'Frisco without touching any other port?

LARSEN:
(slowly)
Yes, Miss Webster—this is a sealing schooner...We make our catch and go home.

Ruth's face turns white at this news. She looks desperately around as though looking for something to cling to.

LARSEN:
(quickly)
What's wrong, Miss Webster?

RUTH:
Nothing...I—I—feel a little dizzy. I guess I'm—I'm not as strong as I thought I was...

LOUIE:
(he pulls out a gold watch proudly)
You've been out too long. You shouldn't be out more than five minutes at the most. You've got to obey my orders.[61]
(he extends his arm)
Come...I'll take you back.
(she takes his arm)

> RUTH:
> *(to Larsen)*
> Excuse me.
>
> LARSEN:
> That's quite all right.[62]

They start to go. He calls after them.

> LARSEN:
> Miss Webster...
> *(she turns)*
> Your accommodations...are they satisfactory?
>
> RUTH:
> *(in a last weak effort to maintain her pose)*
> Yes...thank you...quite...

168. REVERSE ANGLE   SHOOTING FROM LARSEN'S ANGLE
as the two of them start walking away from Larsen. They are a pathetic pair; Louie strutting along in his new dignity, Ruth clattering in her ridiculously high-heeled shoes, trying to keep her footing against the rocking of the boat.

> LARSEN:
> *(shouting)*
> Cooky...[63] I want you to do everything to make Miss Webster feel at home...
> *(cruelly)*
> Put some bars on her window.

Ruth wheels around. Her whole face drops. A look of savage fury comes over it. Suddenly Larsen can contain himself no longer. He begins to roar with laughter. His laughter is the signal for the others; the whole crew, both sailors and hunters alike are doubled up.

168a. CLOSE SHOT   LEACH
as his face goes livid with anger at this action of Larsen's.

169. CLOSE SHOT   RUTH AND LOUIE
Louie looks at her pathetically. He shrugs his shoulders and

turns away from her. The struggle between her desire to cry and her anger is apparent on her face. Suddenly she moves towards the group. CAMERA TRUCKS with her as she goes over to Van Weyden.

170. MEDIUM CLOSE   RUTH AND VAN WEYDEN   OTHERS IN B.G.
Gone is her pose and pretense. She is now the person she really is. She stands facing Van Weyden, her feet spread apart, her arms on her hips. Larsen watches the scene with keen enjoyment.

> **RUTH:**
> So you couldn't keep your mouth shut?
> *(Van Weyden doesn't answer. She screams)*
> Could you?
> *(he still doesn't answer. She slaps him full in the face)*
> Maybe that'll make you answer me...
>
> **VAN WEYDEN:**
> *(his tone sad)*
> You spoke about your past while you were unconscious...you were overheard...
>
> **RUTH:**
> I don't believe you...I don't believe you. You deliberately told them...
>
> **VAN WEYDEN:**
> I swear it's true.

171. WIDER ANGLE
as she suddenly turns to Larsen.

> **RUTH:**
> All right...I lied to you. I put on an act...you had your laugh. You'll give me a break, won't you, Skipper?
>
> **LARSEN:**
> What do you want me to do?
>
> **RUTH:**
> There must be boats passing on the way to China...put me aboard one of them...

LARSEN:
Lady, I been tryin' my best all the voyage to stay clear of boats.

171a. CLOSE SHOT   LEACH
On his face is his pity for Ruth.

RUTH'S VOICE:
Or an island...you could put me ashore on an island. I read some place that the Pacific is full of them...some place where boats pull in. I'll make my way from there.

171b. MEDIUM CLOSE   RUTH AND LARSEN   GROUP IN B.G.

LARSEN:
Louie...take her below...

LOUIE:
You'd better come along...

RUTH:
No...no...[64]
(she looks around at the others)
You all look like pretty decent fellows...like you been in spots like this before.

There is a stony silence. She turns back to Larsen. The intensity in her voice has now changed to outright pleading.

RUTH:
Gimme a break, will you, Skipper? You won't be sorry.
(her attempt to put a seductive tone in her voice is pathetic)
I promise you won't...

LARSEN:
You're not on the streets of the Barbary Coast now. You're on board my vessel. You behave yourself, or you'll spend the rest of the voyage locked below.

171c. CLOSE SHOT LEACH
His eyes are now blazing with anger. It is evident that at any moment he will lose control of himself.

RUTH'S VOICE:
(o.s.)
I didn't mean it that way, Skipper...honest, I didn't.
(the pleading note comes back into her voice)
Don't hold it against me...please...please...give me a break...

Leach, who by this time is no longer able to control his fury at her humiliation, steps forward and goes over to her.

172.   MEDIUM CLOSE   LEACH AND RUTH

LEACH:
(his eyes flashing)
Don't beg! You hear me! Don't beg!!

RUTH:
(turning on Leach)
Beg?! I'd crawl on my knees over every inch of this deck...I'd do anything...anything...not to have to go back...do you know what it's like to be in jail...?

LEACH:
(his voice full of pity and terror)
Yeah...I know what it's like...
(he turns to Larsen)
It ain't enough you knock her down...you gotta kick her too.
(he turns back to Ruth)
Come on, I'll take you back to your cabin.

RUTH:
(shaking his arm from her)
Leave me alone...

She walks a few feet, then suddenly she falls to her knees and begins to sob. Leach goes over to her. He stands over her, looking down at this pathetic spectacle. Then he looks over at Larsen. An insane look of fury comes into his face. Quickly he reaches for a marlin spike and with all his might, throws it at the retreating figure of Larsen.

173. CLOSE   VAN WEYDEN
as he shrieks out involuntarily.[65]

> **VAN WEYDEN:**
> Look out!!

174. CLOSE   LARSEN
as he instinctively ducks his head. The marlin spike whistles past his head and buries itself into the mast. Larsen turns around and walks back toward Leach.

175. MEDIUM GROUP SHOT
as Larsen approaches Leach.

> **LARSEN:**
> Mr. Leach...according to the laws of the sea, I could have you hung for that. But I won't. You're going to save me that trouble. By the time this voyage is over, you'll hang yourself.
> *(he turns to the men)*
> Take him below.

Leach tries to make a dash for Larsen. But before he can go very far, one of the mates slugs him from behind and he slumps to the deck. They drag him off. There is a pause. Suddenly Louie goes over to Ruth and offers her his arm. She shakes it off.

> **RUTH:**
> *(accusingly)*
> You should've let me die...you should've let me die...

She runs into her cabin. There is a long pause. Larsen turns to the men.

> **LARSEN:**
> Get to your work!

The men slowly return to their posts. CAMERA TRUCKS WITH Larsen as he goes up to the bridge.

176. MEDIUM CLOSE   AT BRIDGE   SHOOTING TOWARDS DECK[66]
as Larsen turns suddenly and shouts down,

>**LARSEN:**
>Van Weyden!!

Van Weyden steps forward.

>**LARSEN:**
>Come into my cabin. I want to talk to you.

He turns and walks into his quarters. Van Weyden looks around, then starts forward.

177. INTERIOR   LARSEN'S CABIN   MEDIUM SHOT
as Van Weyden enters. Larsen is seated at a table. There is a bottle and some glasses on it. Van Weyden approaches the table.

>**LARSEN:**
>Sit down...have a drink.

It is evident that Van Weyden, as he sits down, is still shaken by what has happened. Larsen shoves the glass in front of him. Van Weyden takes it and downs it with one gulp.

>**LARSEN:**
>You drank that like you needed it.

Van Weyden doesn't answer. He just sits there looking at Larsen. There is a pause.

>**LARSEN:**
>I suppose I ought to thank you for saving my life.

>**VAN WEYDEN:**
>*(he speaks crisply, his hatred evident)*
>It was instinctive.

>**LARSEN:**
>You sound like you're sorry.

Van Weyden doesn't answer. There is another pause.

LARSEN:
You don't have to work in the galley any more. There's a bunk in the officers' quarters.

VAN WEYDEN:
I prefer to stay with the men.

LARSEN:
(smiling)
I don't think they'll have you after today. You see, their instincts are a little different than yours. They *wanted* Leach to hit me on the head with that spike.
(he shakes his head sadly)
You're in a bad way, Van Weyden...sort of in the middle.

VAN WEYDEN:
At least there's nothing on my conscience.

Larsen roars with laughter.

LARSEN:
You don't suppose there's anything on mine, do you?

178. OMITTED[67]

179. TIGHT TWO SHOT
as the two men stand facing each other across the table. On Van Weyden's face comes a cold, hard smile.

VAN WEYDEN:
Captain Larsen, a few weeks ago, you were interested in this book I intended writing. You were very concerned with how I portrayed you to the world...
(he is digging the words in)
Would you like to hear, Captain Larsen, my description of you?...

LARSEN:
(his eyes alight)
Yeah...sure...go ahead.

> **VAN WEYDEN:**
> It isn't on paper yet...but I know each word of it.
> *(he pauses)*
> I'll skip the physical description...that's obvious.
>
> **LARSEN:**
> *(eagerly)*
> Yeah...yeah...
>
> **VAN WEYDEN:**
> *(he plays with every word)*
> The first impression one gets is that here is a man, no...a brute, completely without feeling or thought...

180. CLOSE SHOT LARSEN
as he reacts to Van Weyden's description.

> **VAN WEYDEN'S VOICE:**
> *(o.s.)*
> A cruel, merciless creature...one who kills for the sake of killing...one who tortures for the sake of hearing the anguished cries of his victims...

Larsen's face goes hard.

> **VAN WEYDEN'S VOICE:**
> But as that first impression wears off, one realizes that this is a highly complex individual.

Larsen's face relaxes.

181. TIGHT TWO SHOT VAN WEYDEN AND LARSEN FAVORING VAN WEYDEN

> **VAN WEYDEN:**
> *(continuing)*
> A mass of contradictions...a man who is tortured by a brain he never should have been given...for with that brain he is able to see clearly that all these things he denies in other men...the need for respect, for dignity ...exist in himself...
> *(he pauses)*

LARSEN:
(tensely)
Go on...you started...finish.

VAN WEYDEN:
(his words come faster)
The reason for his actions then becomes obvious. Since he has found it so difficult in the outside world to maintain that dignity...he creates a world for himself...a ship on which he alone can be master...on which he alone can rule...
(pauses again)

Larsen leans forward. Van Weyden speaks slowly.

VAN WEYDEN:
The next step is a simple one. An ego such as this must constantly be fed...must constantly be reassured of its supremacy...so it feeds itself upon the degradation of people who have never known anything but degradation...it is cruel to people who have never known anything but cruelty...
(Van Weyden's voice is taut)
But to dare to expose that ego in a world where it would meet its equal...

LARSEN:
(shouting)
It's a lie!...
(he pounds the table)
It's a lie!...

Suddenly o.s. is HEARD the SOUND of a door opening. They both turn toward the door.

182. CLOSE SHOT   DOOR   LOUIE
framed in the doorway, still wearing his new clothes, he stands there, nervously polishing his pince-nez glasses.

183. WIDER ANGLE
as he timidly approaches Larsen.

LARSEN:
What do you want?

LOUIE:
(pointing to his clothes)
I want you to forbid the men to laugh at me.[68]

Larsen looks at him in amazement. Louie continues.

LOUIE:
Like Cooky...when I first came on board[69] today. He thought it was funny that I should be wearing these clothes.
(he shakes his head)
But it's not funny at all. When I had my practice, I had twenty suits like this, each one of them was more expensive than the other.
(he straightens proudly)
When I came into the hospital, everybody would greet me with respect...I was a person of importance.

LARSEN:
Yes?...[70]

LOUIE:
I'd like to feel that way again. I don't want the men to call me Louie. I want them to say "Doctor." After all, I did save this woman's life...I did show a certain amount of skill...
(he draws himself up proudly)

>   I haven't had a drink in a week.
>   *(holding out his hand)*
>   See...my hand...it's as steady as a rock.
>   *(to Larsen)*
>   Do you see what I'm trying to get at?
>   *(Larsen is silent)*
>   I probably don't have much more to go. I'm pretty old. My liver's eaten away by liquor.[71] I know I'll never go back to private practice again. I'll probably die a ship's doctor...
>   *(suddenly, intensely)*
>   But whatever time I have left...I'd like to be treated with respect...like I used to be.

There is a pause. Larsen looks at Van Weyden. He smiles, turns back to Louie.

>   **LARSEN:**
>   *(suddenly)*
>   All right, Louie...come with me. I'll tell the men.[72]
>
>   **LOUIE:**
>   *(grabbing his hand, and shaking it)*
>   You're a great man, Wolf[73] Larsen...I'll never forget you for this...never.

Larsen escorts Louie out. Van Weyden, amazed, follows.

184.   MEDIUM SHOT   THE BRIDGE
       as Larsen and Louie emerge, followed by Van Weyden.

>   **LARSEN:**
>   *(shouting down)*
>   Pipe all hands aft!

A shrill sound of the bosun's whistle is HEARD.

185.   ANGLE SHOT   SHOOTING DOWN FROM BRIDGE
       as the men assemble, staring upwards in wonderment at what this new turn of events will lead to.

186. MEDIUM CLOSE   BRIDGE
as Larsen stands there. Next to Larsen stands Louie, beaming. Larsen lays a paternal hand on Louie's shoulder.[74]

> **LARSEN:**
> Listen everybody! Louie's not being treated the way he should be.

Over the men's faces comes a look of complete bewilderment.

> **LOUIE:**
> *(tugging at his sleeve, whispering)*
> Not Louie...Doctor...Doctor...Prescott...Louis J. Prescott.

> **LARSEN:**
> Dr. Prescott...He's to be given all the courtesy and respect due a physician of his standing.
> *(he turns to Louie)*
> Is that satisfactory, Dr. Prescott?

> **LOUIE:**
> Quite...Thank you, Captain Larsen, thank you.

Louie bows curtly to Larsen, bows to Van Weyden and begins to walk toward the steps, looking neither to the right nor to the left of him, his head held high, proud of his new position. Larsen looks at Van Weyden, smiles, then quickly kicks Louie who goes tumbling down the steps.

187. THE MEN
as Louie falls into their midst. A howl of glee goes up from all of them. All the tension that has existed on board up to now gives vent in their desire to have fun with Louie. They surround him.

> **LOUIE:**
> *(backing away)*
> Get away from me! Get away from me!

A sailor walks up to him and takes hold of his lapel.

SAILOR:
It's a nice suit you're wearing Dr. Prescott.
(he rips the lapel)

Another sailor takes the glasses off Louie's nose and stamps on them. A general melee begins. Each one of the sailors is anxious to get a piece of Louie's clothes for a souvenir. By some miracle Louie manages to escape the crowd. He dashes down the deck, his coat tail streaming behind him, followed by the sailors. He reaches the mast where he finds himself surrounded. Suddenly, like a monkey, he begins to clamber up the mast with several of the sailors at his heels. OVER SHOT comes the laughter and cries of the men.

188. MEDIUM CLOSE   VAN WEYDEN AND LARSEN   ON BRIDGE
as they stand watching the scene, Larsen laughing, Van Weyden's face white with apprehension for Louie's safety

189. CLOSE SHOT   TOP OF THE MAST
as Louie hangs precariously, kicking desperately with his feet at the clutching hands from below that seek to pull him down.

190. MEDIUM CLOSE   AT BRIDGE   LARSEN AND VAN WEYDEN

>   **VAN WEYDEN:**
>   He's an old man. He's liable to lose his balance. Let him come down!
>
>   **LARSEN:**
>   Let him beg first. By the time he comes off that mast, he'll be the old Louie again. He'll forget all about his ideas of dignity and respect. He'll kiss every inch of this deck...just glad to be alive.[75]

191. CLOSE SHOT   LOUIE ON THE MAST
his foot still threshing furiously at sailors. He succeeds in kicking one on the hand, who lets go with a yell of pain.

192. MEDIUM CLOSE   THE BRIDGE
as Larsen walks toward the rail.

86 *The Sea Wolf*

> **LARSEN:**
> *(shouting)*
> All right...let him alone...that's enough!
> *(he shouts up)*
> All right, Louie...you can come down now.

193. CLOSE SHOT   LOUIE
He still clings to top of mast. A transformation takes place on his features. The cringing look is gone. Over his face comes a look of stern resolution. His features harden. For the first time, his eyes are deep with purpose.

> **LOUIE:**
> *(shouting)*
> Come down to what?[76]
> *(looks down contemptuously at deck below—spits)*
> You!...
> *(shouts at the men)*
> You below there! You can go on living like mangy curs, but not Louie...
> *(he catches himself)*
> Not Dr. Prescott. I've had my fill. I'll come down the way I want to!

194. CLOSE SHOT   THE BRIDGE

> **LARSEN:**
> *(shouting)*
> Come down, Louie!

195. CLOSE SHOT   TOP OF MAST

> **LOUIE:**[77]
> *(shaking his fist defiantly at Larsen)*
> You'll regret the day you tried to make a fool of Louie!!
> *(shouts down again at the men)*
> Ask him why it is this boat don't sail the regular ship lanes...why she scurries like a rat at sight of another boat...why those hunters he's got down there walk around with loaded guns.

A Screenplay   87

196. MEDIUM CLOSE   LARSEN ON BRIDGE
Larsen's face grows tense.

> **LARSEN:**
> Louie, come down!!

197. CLOSE SHOT   TOP OF MAST

> **LOUIE:**
> *(to Larsen)*
> When I'm good and ready...You won't answer any of these questions, will you, Larsen? Well, I will...
> *(to the men)*
> This ship is a scavenger and he, Larsen, is the worst scavenger of them all! Sealing vessel!...sure there'll be skins of seals on board this boat...but it'll be the skins he steals from other men...from his brother...from his *own* brother...Sure, I know...stealin' doesn't mean anything to men like you...but losin' your lives does...and that's the price he's gonna pay for those skins...*your* lives. There'll be less of you that come back alive from this voyage than went on it. I can promise you that.
> *(to Larsen)*
> Tell them, Larsen...! Tell them about your brother..."*Death*" Larsen. Tell them about the fear that comes into your heart at the mention of his name...

198. CLOSE SHOT   LARSEN AT BRIDGE

> **LARSEN:**
> *(rapidly losing his control)*
> I fear no man...no man...

199. CLOSE SHOT   LOUIE
Now that he has the bit in his teeth he is riding high.

> **LOUIE:**
> Go ahead, Larsen, tell them about your brother...tell them about the oath he's taken to kill you...tell them about his ship, the "Macedonia"...tell them about the

cannon he has on board it, primed to blow you, your ship and all on board to kingdom come...
(he pauses)
He didn't tell you any of that...no...What does he care about your lives? You're not men in his eyes...you're dogs.
(he laughs madly)
And if you as much as raise your voices sayin' you got a right to die your own way, those gunmen of his'll shoot you down like dogs. I know...I've sailed this ship before.

There is a silence.

200. MEDIUM GROUP SHOT   THE SAILORS   SHOOTING TOWARD BRIDGE
as they turn slowly, their faces filled with hatred toward Larsen. There is a tense pause. O.S. comes:

>   **LOUIE'S VOICE:**
>   Hey, everybody, look!!

201. CLOSE SHOT   LOUIE   ON TOP OF MAST
Louie has regained control of himself. He carefully adjusts his disarrayed apparel, straightens his tie, fixes his cuffs, then stands erect on the cross tree, trying to maintain a precarious balance.

201a. CLOSE SHOT   VAN WEYDEN
as the cry freezes on his lips.

202. ANGLE SHOT   SHOOTING PAST MAST
as Louie's body goes hurtling through space and hits the deck with a sickening thud.

203. CLOSE SHOT   AT BRIDGE   LARSEN AND VAN WEYDEN
Van Weyden turns slowly to Larsen and looks at him accusingly. There is a pause.

>   **VAN WEYDEN:**
>   *(repeating)*
>   There is a price that no man will pay for living.

LARSEN:
(quickly, angrily)
It was an accident...he slipped.

Larsen turns and walks back into his cabin as Van Weyden stands there looking after him.

FADE OUT.

FADE IN

203a. INTERIOR   HOLD MEDIUM SHOT
Dark, heavy shadows . . . the faint creaking of the ship. The hatch opens to throw a strong shaft of light into the hold. We see Ruth, silhouetted against the hatchway.

203b. MEDIUM CLOSE   RUTH
In her hands she carries a small bundle wrapped in a handkerchief. She looks about, her big frightened eyes searching the shadows. Finally she sees:

203c. MEDIUM SHOT   LEACH
or what's left of him . . . a heap of flesh and clothes huddled against some barrels. He is like a sick animal hiding either to die or get well. The shaft of light cuts into the scene but Leach is just in the shadows. As we hear Ruth walk toward Leach, Leach slowly turns around to laboriously sit up, his body tense, fists clenched, barely able to move and yet snarling defiance. His defiance changes to a kind of savage anger as Ruth comes into scene. Slowly Ruth kneels beside him. CAMERA FOLLOWS HER into a CLOSE TWO SHOT. She stares wide-eyed at Leach. Her strange attitude, her silence rob him of his defiance, rouses him to a kind of desperation.

LEACH:
(his words biting)
What do you want?

RUTH:
Your friend Mr. Johnson...told me where you were, what they did to you, how they beat you—

There is a pause. He looks at her suspiciously.

>**RUTH:**
>I came to see if there was anything I could do...to help...
>
>**LEACH:**
>*(turning away from her)*
>I don't need no help. I'll take care of myself...I always have...I always will...Now, leave me alone.
>
>**RUTH:**
>*(extending the bundle)*
>I brought you somethin'...a drink, some cigarettes.[78]
>
>**LEACH:**
>*(his voice rising)*
>I said leave me alone.
>
>**RUTH:**
>*(her patience snaps. She blurts out the words)*
>It wasn't my fault...nobody asked you to play hero for me...
>
>**LEACH:**
>Shut up. Nobody's blamin' you...and don't get any ideas in your head either about why I went after Larsen...I can't stand to see a dog beg...

203d. MEDIUM CLOSE SHOT   RUTH
as she reacts to the contempt in Leach's voice.

>**LEACH'S VOICE:**
>*(o.s.)*
>...no less a human bein'...
>*(a pause)*
>Now beat it...

She stands there.

>**LEACH'S VOICE:**
>I said beat it...

> **RUTH:**
> *(slowly)*
> I guess that's how you'd talk to a dog, too...[79]

203e. MEDIUM CLOSE
as Ruth makes a motion as though to leave him.

> **LEACH:**
> *(contritely)*
> I'm sorry I said that...
> *(intensely)*
> I hadda let my hate out on someone. You happened to come along...
> *(tensely)*
> Didn't you ever feel that way?

She looks at him for an instant, then slowly turns and starts walking away from him. Realizing that he has not succeeded, he tries to get up and stop her from going, but the effort is too much for him. He goes a few steps then collapses in a heap on the floor.

203f. WIDER ANGLE
as Ruth quickly turns. A look of anxiety comes over her face. She walks quickly toward Leach, kneels down and bends over him. Her eyes search his face and notice the look of pain on it.

> **RUTH:**
> You're hurt bad.

> **LEACH:**
> *(it is an effort for him to speak)*
> Yeah...Larsen does a good job.

> **RUTH:**
> *(as she props his coat under his head)*
> Here...lie down...rest...close your eyes...try to sleep.[80]

> **LEACH:**
> *(shaking his head)*
> No...I tried that...it's no good. When I close my eyes I

see Larsen grinnin' at me...laughin' at me...I wake up tryin' to wipe that grin off his face. When I keep my eyes open...my head's clearer. I can think about what I'm gonna do...
(suddenly)
That drink.[81]

She hurriedly undoes the knot of the bundle, takes out a flask and hands it to him. With trembling hands, he takes the flask from her and drinks. After a while he puts down the flask, wipes his mouth with the back of his hand, heaving a sigh of relief. Again he turns to her.

LEACH:
... the cigarettes.

She hands him the cigarettes and a match. With shaking hands, he strikes the match, throwing into bold relief both their faces. As he does so, Ruth also takes a cigarette.

RUTH:
Hold that light.[82]

He holds the light for her. She lights up, then blows out the match. They are in semi-darkness except for the shaft of light coming into the hold and the glow of their cigarettes. For an instant they sit there puffing away at their cigarettes, neither of them saying a word. Suddenly from a distance comes the sweet strains of a harmonica, playing a mournful tune.

A Screenplay

203g. TIGHT TWO SHOT
as the two of them listen to the strains of the harmonica for a while. (NOTE: All through the rest of this scene the strains of the harmonica are HEARD.)

> **LEACH:**
> That's the kid. Whenever he feels sad...he plays that harmonica...he makes up the songs. He's good, ain't he? Listen...
> *(again they listen)*
> I guess he's playin' that one for Louie.

There is a pause.

> **RUTH:**
> *(a sad note in her voice)*
> Louie...I liked Louie. He was decent.
>
> **LEACH:**
> Fat old drunken Louie...He was so proud of them fancy clothes of his, too...poor Louie.
>
> **RUTH:**
> Lucky Louie...
>
> **LEACH:**
> *(quickly)*
> I don't think so.
>
> **RUTH:**
> It's over for him. All the heartaches and the pain.
>
> **LEACH:**
> *(suddenly)*
> Supposin' I said to you I can get you off this boat...
>
> **RUTH:**
> Supposin' I said to you it don't make any difference to me, anymore.
>
> **LEACH:**
> *(there is a pause in his voice)*

You won't have to go back to the States. There's an iron gate there waitin' to shut behind me, too.

RUTH:
Inside or outside...it's all the same. To be free...to be let alone...to live in peace...even if it's only for a little while...I don't expect that anymore.

LEACH:
You gotta fight...you can't quit...Tomorrow I'll be on my feet...tomorrow—

RUTH:
Will be like today...and the day before...He'll beat you again...

LEACH:
(a look of hate on his face)
What I got inside of me Larsen can't get at...that's what drives him crazy.

RUTH:
(desperately)
What...what is it?

LEACH:
(his voice tortured)
I don't know...I can't explain it...it's just somethin' that tells me to go on fightin'...that tells me that there's somethin' for people like us...

RUTH:
(looking into his eyes for the first time)
Like us?

There is a pause.

LEACH:
Yeah...like us...Men like Larsen can't keep on grindin' us down because we're nobodies. That ain't true...we're somebodies...
(suddenly)
I got a plan...all worked out in my mind. I'll get even with Larsen. We'll get off this boat...

RUTH:
(slowly)
We?

LEACH:
Yeah...we...you...me...and anybody else who wants to go. We'll all be free...if it works...

RUTH:
(slowly)
And if it don't...
(pauses)
You might be killed...

LEACH:
(shrugging his shoulders)
You said it yourself before...what have we got to lose?

Suddenly her lips begin to quiver as though she were trying to stop herself from crying, but the effort is too difficult. Low, strangled sobs come out of her in spite of herself.[83]

LEACH:
(noticing this)
What're you cryin' about? You scared?

RUTH:
(suddenly)
Yeah...but not for myself.
(she blurts the words out)
For you.

203h. WIDER ANGLE
as she suddenly turns and runs, stumbling out of the hold into the corridor. CAMERA MOVES INTO A:

203i. CLOSE SHOT   LEACH
as he sits there staring after her, the limp cigarette still in his lips, a troubled look in his eyes. OVER SCENE comes the soft strains of the harmonica still being played, as we

FADE OUT.

FADE IN

204. INTERIOR GALLEY   CLOSE SHOT   COOKY   NIGHT[84]
as he lies stirring restlessly in his bunk. He awakens and sits up, a look of disgust on his face. He sits and listens. O.S. as though from a far distance comes the faint SOUND of a woman's sobbing. Another look of disgust comes upon Cooky's face. He looks over to the other side of the room. CAMERA PANS with his gaze to:

205. CLOSE SHOT   VAN WEYDEN
as he too lies awake, listening to the SOUND of the sobbing. On his face is a look of pity.

> **COOKY'S VOICE:**
> *(o.s.)*
> Cryin'…cryin'…cryin'…all night she's been lyin' there cryin'…she might as well shut up…'twon't do 'er no good.

206. MEDIUM SHOT   GALLEY   COOKY AND VAN WEYDEN
The sobbing suddenly stops.

> **COOKY:**
> She's stopped now. I 'ope she don't start again.

A deathly quiet seems to hang over the room. Both Cooky and Van Weyden lie there silently.

> **COOKY:**
> *(he leans over confidentially)*
> Leach was in to see 'er this evenin'…'e st'yed several 'ours.
> *(he winks broadly)*

207. REVERSE ANGLE   COOKY
as he smiles gleefully.

> **COOKY:**
> Wot a beatin' Leach took from Larsen…the bloodiest

and most artistic h't's ever been my pleasure to
witness.
(he demonstrates)
'E'd knock 'im down...then 'e'd lift 'im up again...'e'd
knock 'im down...then 'e'd lift him up again...an' the
blood kept flowin' from 'is nose like the spout from a
whale. I been 'avin' pleasant dreams abaht it all night.

Again there is a silence. Cooky takes out a cigarette, lights it nervously.

COOKY:
I got the cold shivers tonight...I swear I 'ave. All night
I been 'earin' the strangest kind of noises, voices whisperin'...footsteps...

Another pause. They both listen tensely.

COOKY:
(confidentially to Van Weyden)
Orful quiet, ain't it?...I ain't 'eard a sound from the
foc'sle all night. There's somethin' brewin' aboard this
ship. I can feel it in my bones.
(he puffs on his cigarette nervously)
The men are in an awful ugly mood...
(he takes another puff)
Oh well...hit's no skin off my back...I'm snug and safe
in my little bunk...

He continues to puff nervously on his cigarette.

207b. MEDIUM CLOSE SHOT   QUARTERDECK   NIGHT
Johnson is at the wheel. He keeps looking nervously about him.
Suddenly the SOUND of a man's feet is HEARD coming up from
Larsen's cabin. Johnson looks o.s. and waves his hand quickly.

207c. TIGHT TWO SHOT   LEACH AND HARRISON
They crouch, hidden in the shadows of the mainmast next to
the hatch. Leach waves his hand quickly in return. He looks at
Harrison. Both men crouch a little lower, like runners about to
get off their mark.

207d. MEDIUM CLOSE   QUARTERDECK
as Larsen approaches Johnson. On Larsen's face is a look of intense pain.

> **JOHNSON:**
> *(quietly)*
> Mr. Svenson was just looking for you, sir.
>
> **LARSEN:**
> Svenson? What did he want?
>
> **JOHNSON:**
> *(quickly)*
> I don't know, sir. I just saw him going down towards the foc'sle.

Johnson points off in the direction of Leach and Harrison. Larsen starts to go, then turns and stops.

> **LARSEN:**
> *(suspiciously)*
> Why are you taking this watch alone?
>
> **JOHNSON:**
> *(quickly)*
> Harrison wasn't feeling well, sir.

There is a pause.

> **LARSEN:**
> *(it is evident he is nervous)*
> All right

He turns and walks toward the foc'sle.

207e. MEDIUM CLOSE   SHOOTING PAST LEACH AND HARRISON
as they crouch waiting for Larsen to approach. Just as he is about to descend, he stops.

207f. CLOSE SHOT   LARSEN AT RAIL
He rubs the palm of his hand into his forehead as though trying

to rub out the pain. There is a tortured expression on his face.
Suddenly we HEAR:

> **SVENSON'S VOICE:**
> They're getting worse, ain't they, sir?[85]

Larsen wheels quickly.

207g. WIDER ANGLE   SHOOTING TOWARD SVENSON
He walks down the deck toward Svenson.

> **LARSEN:**
> *(viciously)*
> I didn't ask you for your opinion.[86]

There is a pause.

> **LARSEN:**
> Johnson said you were looking for me.[87]

> **SVENSON:**
> *(a bit bewildered)*
> I didn't want to see you.[88]

207h. CLOSE SHOT   LEACH AND HARRISON
Before another word can be uttered, the figures of Leach and Harrison spring out of the darkness at Larsen and Svenson, forcing them both to the deck.

207j. CLOSE SHOT   JOHNSON AT WHEEL
as he stands there, staring straight ahead of him, the expression on his face giving no indication of the struggle that is being waged below. A few heavy thuds are HEARD. There is a pause, then a SPLASH, then another SPLASH. Johnson nods his head in grave disapproval.

208. MEDIUM SHOT   INTERIOR GALLEY   VAN WEYDEN AND COOKY
as Van Weyden suddenly throws the covers off and gets out of bed. He puts on his coat and starts for the door.

> **COOKY:**
> An' where is it ye think yer goin'?
>
> **VAN WEYDEN:**
> To take a walk on deck...I can't sleep.
>
> **COOKY:**
> Sensitive soul...ain't you?

Van Weyden starts walking up the steps.

> **COOKY:**
> Careful on deck that the ghost of Louie don't come jumpin' down at ye from the mainmast.

His cackle follows Van Weyden out. Suddenly the sobbing begins again.[89]

> **COOKY:**
> Shut up...d'ye 'ear me?...shut up! I'm an 'ard workin' man...I need me sleep...shut up!!

He picks up a shoe and hurls it against the wall.

209. MEDIUM CLOSE   CORRIDOR
as Van Weyden makes his way along it. Passing Ruth's cabin, he hesitates. The sobbing still continues. He lifts his hand as though to knock on the door, when suddenly the SOUNDS of footsteps coming down the corridor are HEARD. He turns quickly.

210. REVERSE ANGLE
Out of the shadows from the direction of the deck Leach appears. His face is a horrible mass of bruises and he is almost swollen beyond recognition. His eyes are half closed, filled with a sort of madness. Behind him is Harrison. Leach stops in front of Van Weyden.

211. TIGHT TWO SHOT   LEACH AND VAN WEYDEN
as Leach places his back against the door and stands there glaring at Van Weyden. He nods to Harrison who nods back and

passes the two men, then disappears in the direction of the bunkhouse.

> LEACH:
> What do you want?
>
> VAN WEYDEN:
> I wanted to talk to her...
>
> LEACH:
> Leave her alone!
>
> VAN WEYDEN:
> I heard her crying...
>
> LEACH:
> *(bitterly)*
> You heard her cryin' on the deck too.
>
> VAN WEYDEN:
> There was nothing I could do.
>
> LEACH:
> Well, there's nothing you can do now.
> *(strangely)*
> What had to be done has been done.

Van Weyden looks at him.

> VAN WEYDEN:
> Leach...believe me...I'd like to help you.
>
> LEACH:
> We don't need your help.
>
> VAN WEYDEN:
> *We?*...
>
> LEACH:
> *(he says the word, possessively, defiantly)*
> Yeah...we. All we gotta do to get off this boat is flap our wings and fly away.
> *(bitterly)*

> Yeah...we got wings—jailbirds' wings. Goodnight, Van Weyden.

There is a pause. Van Weyden looks at him strangely.

> **VAN WEYDEN:**
> Goodnight, Leach.

Van Weyden turns and walks toward the deck. Leach stands there for a while, listening to his footsteps. As they die down, he looks around the corridor quickly, then he raps softly on Ruth's door. There is no answer at first. He raps again once, twice. Suddenly we HEAR:

> **RUTH'S VOICE:**
> Yes...who is it?
>
> **LEACH:**
> It's me.

The door opens slightly.

212. TIGHT TWO SHOT   AT DOOR   SHOOTING FROM LEACH'S ANGLE TOWARD RUTH
    The only glimpse we have of her is through the half open door.[90]

> **LEACH:**
> You can stop your cryin' now.

She looks up at him quickly, her face tense. A wild exultant look comes into Leach's eyes. He speaks hoarsely, like a man who has just experienced a terrific emotion.

> **LEACH:**
> It's over...it's done with.

She looks at him for an instant as though disbelieving.

> **LEACH:**
> Don't you understand me...it's over...it's done with.

Slowly her knees begin to give way. Leach notices this.

LEACH:
Steady...there's no time for that now.

RUTH:
I'll be all right.

LEACH:
(wild exultation in his voice)
Soon we'll be off this hell ship...we'll forget we ever were on board it...

RUTH:
(pitifully)
When?...when?...

LEACH:
The first chance we get to make a break for it. It'll be much easier now...[91] a few days...maybe a week. It'll take some time for me and Johnson to load the boat with supplies...we got a long, tough trip ahead of us...fifteen hundred miles in an open boat. But we'll make it...we'll make it, I tell you.

RUTH:
(bitterly)
If I don't jinx you...

LEACH:
(grabbing her arm)
Don't say that...do y'hear me? Don't say that!!

RUTH:
(looking down at her arm where he's holding her)
My arm...you're hurting me.

Leach looks down too.

213. CLOSE SHOT   LEACH'S FINGERS
clutched so strongly on Ruth's bare arm that they leave white streaks as his fingers release their hold.

214. TIGHT TWO SHOT   LEACH AND RUTH

>**LEACH:**
>I didn't mean to grab you so tight. You made me mad.
>*(he looks down again at her, as she holds her arm)*
>That's the arm where they...?
>*(he pauses, a little proudly)*
>My blood...
>
>**RUTH:**
>*(her voice husky)*
>Yeah...*your* blood...

He strokes it for a moment. In his gesture is portrayed all their understanding for each other, all the ties that bind them together.

>**LEACH:**
>*(suddenly)*
>I can't take any more chances. I gotta get back to the bunkhouse. Goodnight...
>*(he starts to go, looks back)*
>No more tears.
>
>**RUTH:**
>*(smiling wanly)*
>No...no more tears.

She closes the door. He disappears into the shadows of the corridor.

215. EXTERIOR   MEDIUM SHOT
as Van Weyden walks along the deck. In the distance can be seen the figure of Johnson. A ship's bell strikes the hour. Van Weyden walks over to the rail and looks out.

216. CLOSE SHOT   VAN WEYDEN
as he stares out at the night . . . a troubled look in his eyes. Suddenly a strange SOUND is HEARD as though someone were scraping the sides of the vessel. He looks off in the direction of the SOUND. His eyes open wide in terror.

217. CLOSE SHOT   THE RAIL
as a sinewy hand appears over the side, clutching the rail . . . then a head, dripping and wet . . . then the face of "Wolf" Larsen. One side of his face is streaked with blood that appears to come from a wound in his head. With a desperate effort he heaves himself over the side of the rail and stands on deck, shaking the water from him and wiping away the blood from his eyes.[92]

218. CLOSE SHOT   JOHNSON
as his eyes open wide in terror at the sight of Larsen on *deck*. He makes a move as though to come down from the bridge.

219. MEDIUM CLOSE   RAIL   LARSEN, VAN WEYDEN   (SHOOTING TOWARD JOHNSON)
as Larsen notices Johnson's move.

> **LARSEN:**
> *(quickly)*
> Stay at that wheel!![93]
> *(he turns to Van Weyden)*
> How long have you been on deck?
>
> **VAN WEYDEN:**
> I just came up.
>
> **LARSEN:**
> Did you see anybody come down...into the foc'sle?

There is a pause.

> **VAN WEYDEN:**
> No, sir.
>
> **LARSEN:**
> *(looking at him)*
> You're probably lying. Come with me.

He walks over to Johnson.

220. MEDIUM CLOSE   AT BRIDGE   JOHNSON
as Larsen and Van Weyden approach him.

LARSEN:
Johnson, you saw what happened on this deck a little while ago.

JOHNSON:
I saw nothing, sir.

LARSEN:
Mr. Svenson and I were slugged and thrown overboard.

JOHNSON:
There's a strong wind.[94] My eyes were on the course.

LARSEN:
Johnson...who did it?

JOHNSON:
I told you, sir...I saw nothing.

LARSEN:
Svenson's probably dead. I'll need a new mate...you can have his job...

JOHNSON:
I would make a bad mate, sir.[95] I don't know how to give orders, sir...only to take them.

LARSEN:
D'ye know how to take a beating?[96]

JOHNSON:
(slowly)
Yes, sir.

Larsen looks at him, then turns to Van Weyden.

LARSEN:
You...come with me.

He starts walking toward the foc'sle, Van Weyden following him.

221. MEDIUM CLOSE   HATCHWAY
as Larsen stops, takes a lamp from the mast and lights it. The

light throws both their faces into grotesque relief. He hands the lamp to Van Weyden.

> **LARSEN:**
> You go down first.[97]
>
> **VAN WEYDEN:**
> You're not going down into the foc'sle?
>
> **LARSEN:**
> Yes.
>
> **VAN WEYDEN:**
> But how will you know who did it?
>
> **LARSEN:**
> Don't worry. I'll know...get a move on.
> *(he shoves Van Weyden ahead of him)*

222. INTERIOR   FOC'SLE
    as first Van Weyden and then Larsen appear. Van Weyden stands there, his terror evident. Larsen looks every inch alert. O.S. come the various SOUNDS of men asleep . . . deep breathing, snoring, etc. Larsen nods his head in the direction of the first bunk. CAMERA MOVES WITH Van Weyden and Larsen as they go over to it. Larsen motions to Van Weyden to lift the lamp higher.

223. CLOSE SHOT   BUNK
    In it lies a seaman, apparently fast asleep. Larsen places his thumb and forefinger on the man's wrist and listens for the beat of his pulse. During this the man awakens gently and stares at Larsen. There is no doubt but that the man really has been asleep. Larsen quickly places his fingers on the seaman's lips, causing him to be quiet, and moves on to another bunk.

224. CLOSE SHOT   ANOTHER BUNK[98]
    as Larsen and Van Weyden approach. In it lies the young boy who was sick on board. His head is thrown back and he seems to be muttering in his sleep. Larsen bends forward to listen to him.

BOY:
I'll never go to sea again...I'll never go to sea again.
(like a prayer)
I hate it...I hate it...

Larsen walks quickly away from him.

225. MEDIUM SHOT   THE BUNKHOUSE
as Larsen walks along the narrow passway, preceded by Van Weyden.

226. CLOSE SHOT   LEACH
as he stealthily raises his head from the upper bunk in which he is sleeping.

227. CLOSE SHOT   HARRISON
in the bunk across the way from Leach's. He nods his head as he sees Leach's signal.

228. MEDIUM SHOT   THE BUNKHOUSE[99]
as Larsen bends down to examine another sailor and Van Weyden stands there with the lamp. Suddenly from up above, Leach springs straight on the back of Larsen. As he does so, Harrison knocks the lamp from the hand of Van Weyden, plunging the bunkhouse into complete darkness. Almost like a signal men come tumbling out of their bunks to join in.

LEACH'S VOICE:
(in the darkness)
It's Larsen! I've got Larsen! A knife! Somebody get me a knife!!

Only movements can be seen in the darkness . . . bodies merged with one another . . . the SOUND of blows . . . the hard breathing of men. It all seems like one huge mass, inch by inch making its way to the foc'sle steps.

LEACH'S VOICE:
(insistently)
A knife! Somebody hand me a knife...I've got him, I tell you...I've got him!!

Suddenly the door opens from above and a swath of moonlight bathes the room, throwing the mass of fighting men into bold relief.

229. CLOSE SHOT   THE MATE
as he peers down into the hold.

> **MATE:**
> Below there! What's going on?

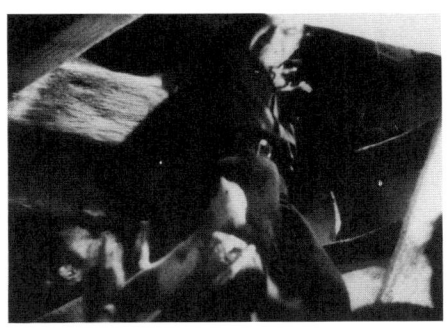

230. MEDIUM CLOSE   THE STAIRWAY
as we see, out of the squirming mass, the figure of Larsen emerges . . . kicking, biting, gouging, pinching, shaking off men, until finally he reaches the top step with only two men clinging still to his heels.

> **LARSEN:**
> It's me...Larsen...

The mate reaches down his hand. Larsen grabs it. Then with a final, desperate, powerful kick, he succeeds in making the top rung. The mate hoists him out of sight, and the door closes behind him, again plunging the room into complete darkness. Somebody strikes a light. The lamp is lit again. CAMERA PANS AROUND the room as it PICKS UP the faces of the men, beaten, bruised and bloody . . . till it COMES TO REST on Leach, sitting on a bunk . . . his eyes smoldering with anger.

231. MEDIUM CLOSE   LEACH
as the men group around him.

HARRISON:
(accusingly)
Now we're in for it...
(suddenly)
You...you put us up to it...it was your idea to push him overboard.

LEACH:[100]
How was I to know he'd come back from the dead...
(suddenly)
If you'd've only handed me a knife...I had him...I had him in my hands, I tell you...once and for all, I would've put an end to him.

HARRISON:
You weren't thinkin' of us when you gave us this idea...you were thinkin' of you and that slug...

Leach slaps the man in the face. Two men jump on him. Harrison steps in between.

YOUNG SAILOR:
(hysterically)
Stop it! There's been enough blood let tonight!! Stop it!!

HARRISON:
(still furious)
Be men, he says...stand up for your rights...stand up for him, he meant.
(he turns to the others)
What difference does it make to us who our master is and what kind of a ship we sail? Get rid of Larsen... there's a dozen Larsens to take his place.

LEACH:
Stop bellyachin'...you shoulda thought of all that before.

HARRISON:
Well, I didn't...I'm thinkin' of it now...
(hysterically)
I'll tell him who put us up to it...I'll tell him.

LEACH:
(springing to his feet)
You don't have to tell him. I'll tell him myself. I'm a man. I'll live like one, and if I have to, I'll go out like Louie...thumbin' my nose at him.
(he looks at them with disgust)
You've forgotten all about Louie, haven't you? You're too busy worryin' about what's gonna happen to you. Well...nothin's gonna happen. He needs you to sail his ship for him...he needs you to break your backs for him...Maybe someday you'll get wise to that.

Suddenly the doorway opens and the voice of the mate shouts down.

MATE'S VOICE:
Van Weyden!!

They all look around. For the first time, they become aware of the fact that he has been there all this time.

232. CLOSE SHOT   VAN WEYDEN
as he stands in the corner of the bunkhouse.

233. WIDER ANGLE
as the men suddenly move toward him, threateningly.

MATE'S VOICE:
(shouting down again)
Van Weyden...are you down there?

A SAILOR:
(quickly)
No...he isn't!

VAN WEYDEN:
(suddenly shouting up)
Yes...yes, I'm here.

MATE'S VOICE:
Well, you better come up quick. The Old Man wants you in his cabin.

Van Weyden starts to go up the stairs. He finds his way blocked by the men.

>**A SAILOR:**
>*(grabbing him)*
>If you so much as open your mouth...
>
>**VAN WEYDEN:**
>I've seen and heard nothing.
>
>**SAILOR:**
>Remember that!

He steps aside. Van Weyden goes up the hatchway.

>**LEACH:**
>*(laughing)*
>Now you guys have got something else to worry about.

DISSOLVE TO:

234. INTERIOR   LARSEN'S CABIN[101]
Larsen is standing in the center of the cabin, stripped to the waist. He is breathing hard from the terrific fight he has just gone through. In his eyes is still the gleam of battle. He is feeling high, exultant. He displays this in every move, every gesture. Van Weyden is applying bandages and tape to the parts of Larsen's body which have been bruised. (MR. WALLIS' NOTE: Be careful of this makeup. Not too much of the coagulated blood.)

>**LARSEN:**
>*(proudly)*
>Twelve of them...twelve men...trying to kill me, and I got out alive!...
>
>**VAN WEYDEN:**
>Next time they might not fail.
>
>**LARSEN:**
>The next time they won't try...
>*(there is no doubt of his pride in his accomplishment)*
>D'ye know how I managed to get back on board? I grabbed a tow line and hoisted myself up inch by

inch...and me with a gash in my head the size of a three penny nail. How many men d'ye know could've done that?...how many men?
(suddenly, like a boy asking for praise)
What did they say back there in the bunkhouse, huh? What did they say?

VAN WEYDEN:
I didn't hear them say a thing.

LARSEN:
You're lyin'...Larsen's a devil, they're sayin'...he's not an ordinary human being. They're right...I'm not.

235. CLOSE SHOT   LARSEN

The old note of justification in front of Van Weyden comes back into his voice.

LARSEN:
I could have been skipper of the sealing fleet instead of my brother...yeah...me. It was offered to me. But I wouldn't have it. It was too easy. What would I have been?...just another cog in a machine...*Captain* Larsen workin' for a group of fat shipowners. Who am I now?..."Wolf" Larsen...stealin' from 'em...makin' 'em pay me for every hard inch of the way. They're afraid of me. They couldn't buy me out like they did my brother.
(bitterly)
May his body soon be rotting at the bottom of the sea.

A knock is HEARD at the door. He bellows out.

LARSEN:
Who is it?

COOKY'S VOICE:
(o.s.)
It's me...Cooky.

236. CLOSE SHOT   DOORWAY
as Cooky appears. He is the picture of contriteness.

COOKY:
I didn't know wot was 'appenin', sir...I was fast asleep. Are yu 'urt bad?

237. WIDER ANGLE
as Cooky comes into the room.

LARSEN:
I beat 'em all, Cooky...I beat 'em all.

COOKY:
Of course ye did, sir...nevertheless, ye shoulda called me...I woulda 'elped ye. I'da given those beggars what for...
(he takes out his knife and demonstrates)
I'da slashed 'em to ribbons for darin' to raise their fingers to the marster...I wish you'da called me.

LARSEN:
(suddenly as Van Weyden tightens the tape)
Careful...

COOKY:
(leaping in and pushing him away)
Ye clumsy lout...
(he takes the tape)
I'll do it for ye, sir...nice an' gentle like.
(he puts the knife down on the table)

238. MEDIUM CLOSE LARSEN AND COOKY
as Cooky starts taping him.

LARSEN:
Cooky...I want the names of all the men who were in on this.

COOKY:
(righteously)
Ye shall 'ave 'em, sir.

LARSEN:
I want to know who was the leader...how the thing

was worked out and what the men intended doing after they got rid of me. D'ye think ye can get all that?

COOKY:
(hurt)
'Ave I ever failed ye, sir?

LARSEN:
(to Van Weyden)
Sterling character, isn't he? That's his profession, being a stool pigeon...cooking's only a hobby.
(he pauses deliberately, a smile comes over his face)
How you could have accused such a character of stealing your money...

COOKY:
(his face is a picture of outraged virtue)
Did 'e s'y that, sir? Oh, the liar...the dirty, snivelin' liar.
(he moves toward Van Weyden)
I dare ye to repeat it to my f'yce.

VAN WEYDEN:
(quietly)
I said you were the only one who could have taken the money.

Cooky's answer is to slap Van Weyden full in the face. Suddenly Van Weyden's face grows livid with rage. Like a snarling, cornered beast, he jumps for Cooky's throat. With one hand on Cooky's throat, he snatches the knife from the table. Cooky's face goes white with fear. That Van Weyden is mad enough to murder is quite evident.

VAN WEYDEN:
(quiet, deadly)
Cooky, if you ever lay a hand on me again, I'll kill you...I swear I will.

LARSEN:
(who has been enjoying this tremendously)
Do it now, Mr. Van Weyden, stick the knife into him. You believe in immortality. Let his spirit free. It may be a beautiful one, just imprisoned in a dirty, ugly carcass. Go ahead, Van Weyden, stick the knife into him.

The taunting words of Larsen seen to make Van Weyden come to his senses. Slowly he releases his clutch on Cooky's throat. Cooky takes advantage of this to dash madly out of the cabin.

239. TWO SHOT   LARSEN AND VAN WEYDEN

LARSEN:[102]
(still taunting him)
Is this the first time you ever wanted to commit a murder?
(Van Weyden doesn't answer)
Good feeling, isn't it...to know that you hold a man's life in your hands. You enjoyed it, didn't you?
(into his eyes comes a demoniacal gleam)

VAN WEYDEN:
I think I know now why men call you "Wolf"...

LARSEN:
You know a lot of things you didn't know before. You've changed, Mr. Van Weyden.

He starts to walk toward Van Weyden who backs away from him, still holding the knife in his hand.

LARSEN:
I told you you would. You're not the fine gentleman you were when you first came on board this boat. You've become more like the rest of them...like me.

> *(mocking him, he recalls their first meeting)*
> "A brutal, calloused and inhuman creature"...

Larsen pauses. Van Weyden's back is against the wall.

> **LARSEN:**
> I bet you'd think nothing now of turning that knife on me if I were to suddenly reach out...
>
> **VAN WEYDEN:**
> You're mad, Larsen...stark, raving mad...
>
> **LARSEN:**
> *(continuing)*
> ...grab you by the throat...
> *(he suits the action to the words)*

Van Weyden slashes furiously at Larsen. Larsen grips his knife hand and twists it mercilessly behind his back. Van Weyden's face contorts with pain. His knees keep giving way as Larsen keeps pressing him toward the floor. Abruptly, Larsen stops. His hands go to his head, a low moan of pain escapes from his lips, almost like the cry of a wounded animal. He stumbles around the room for a few seconds, then finding the edge of a chair, falls down upon it. He keeps his head buried in his hands. His moans continue.

> **VAN WEYDEN:**
> *(going to him)*
> Larsen! What is it?

LARSEN:
Let me alone...let me alone...[103]

There is a long pause. As Van Weyden stands over Larsen, looking at him, the room begins to grow light. It is daybreak. With each passing moment, the room becomes brighter. Larsen doesn't look up. He keeps moaning.

VAN WEYDEN:
What is it?[104]

LARSEN:
Nothing...nothing...it's a headache. I often get them. They come and go.
(his voice tortured)
This pressure on my brain...if it would only go away. It's driving me crazy...

He starts to moan again. Suddenly, o.s. is HEARD the SOUND of four bells.

LARSEN:
Four bells...it ought to be getting light soon.

240. CLOSE SHOT   VAN WEYDEN
as he reacts to this strange statement.

241. MEDIUM CLOSE   LARSEN AND VAN WEYDEN

LARSEN:
Open the curtains, Van Weyden.

Van Weyden stands there looking at him, a growing realization coming over his face.

LARSEN:
Did you hear me, Van Weyden. I said open the curtains.

Van Weyden comes close to him. He passes his hand before Larsen's eyes. There is no reaction. He starts back away from him.

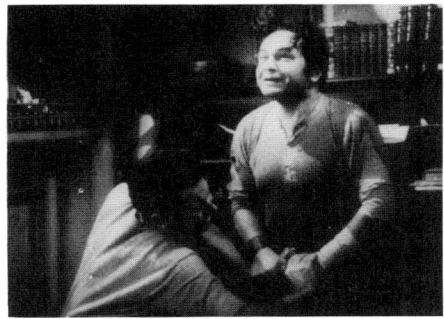

LARSEN:
Van Weyden?...

VAN WEYDEN:
Yes...

LARSEN:
Where're you going?

VAN WEYDEN:
I wasn't going any place.

LARSEN:
You were...don't lie to me...I heard your footsteps.
(terror suddenly comes into your voice)
You know...Van Weyden...you know.

VAN WEYDEN:
Yes, I know.

LARSEN:
You won't tell them?...you won't tell them...
(Van Weyden is silent)
If they find out I'm blind, they'll come up here and murder me...I won't have a chance...
(pleading)
It'll go away...in a little while. It always has...I'll be able to see again. Don't tell them. Don't tell them.

242. CLOSE SHOT VAN WEYDEN
as he stands against the wall, undecided whether to go or to stay. The struggle is reflected on his face.

> **LARSEN'S VOICE:**
> *(o.s.)*
> Pity! Van Weyden...pity!!

Suddenly Van Weyden, despite himself, starts going towards Larsen.

243. MEDIUM CLOSE   LARSEN
As Van Weyden approaches him, a crafty look has come over his face.

> **LARSEN:**[105]
> Closer...closer...come nearer to me...I want to know you're still here.

Van Weyden comes close to him. Suddenly Larsen reaches out and grabs both his hands in an iron vise. He imitates his previous plea.

> **LARSEN:**
> Pity...Van Weyden...pity...
> *(he laughs)*
> You had your chance, you fool, but you lost it...Now you'll have to stay here with me until my sight comes back again...I was wrong, Van Weyden, you haven't changed...you haven't changed a bit...

His laughter continues, as we

FADE OUT.

FADE IN

244. THE DECK   SLOW PANNING SHOT   DAY
CAMERA MOVES SLOWLY about the deck, PICKING UP first the sailors as they stand huddled together, their faces lowered, their expressions sullen. Leach and Johnson stand in the forefront of the group. There is a general air of tension in the scene. Off scene comes the creaking of a man's shoes pacing the deck. The SHOT HOLDS for a few seconds until we get the feeling

that the creaking SOUND of the pacing becomes the rhythmic beat of the scene. CAMERA PICKS UP Cooky, watching the men, a smug, self-complacent and knowing leer on his face. IT MOVES ON to PICK UP the hunters standing off towards the rail, their hands clutching their rifles tightly as though ready to spring into action at a moment's notice. CAMERA MOVES to Ruth as she stands in the hatchway watching the scene. In her eyes is the same anxiety and tension as that of the others. Her fists are tightly clenched and held close to her sides, her eyes half shut. CAMERA MOVES ON to Van Weyden as he stands apart from the rest of the men at the rail. By this time the creaking SOUND of the pacing feet has assumed a monotonous, maddening effect. CAMERA MOVES BACK and HOLDS ON:

245. MEDIUM GROUP SHOT   THE SAILORS
as they stand there like men awaiting the drop of the executioner's axe. Suddenly Leach can take it no longer. He steps forward.

> **LEACH:**
> *(his tenseness reflected in his voice)*
> All right...let's get it over with!

246. CLOSE SHOT   LARSEN   AT BRIDGE
as he suddenly stops his pacing, starts walking in the direction of the men.

247. MEDIUM SHOT   THE DECK
as Larsen walks down the steps leading to the deck and faces the men.

248. MEDIUM CLOSE-LARSEN AND THE MEN

> **LARSEN:**
> *(slowly and with great emphasis)*
> I have here in my pocket a list...
> *(he takes a slip of paper from his pocket and holds it up)*
> A list of the names of all of the men who were part of this plot to kill me. I know exactly how it was started —who led it—and what you intended to do with this

>
> ship after my death.[106] Your plan was to scuttle it and report to the authorities we had been wrecked at sea...[107]
> *(he smiles)*
> An ingenious plan, a daring plan...
> *(he pauses, looks at Leach)*
> If it had succeeded, Mr. Leach. You had other plans too, didn't you, Mr. Leach?
> *(he waves his hand as though vaguely trying to remember)*
> Something about escaping in a boat...

Leach looks off quickly.

249. CLOSE SHOT   RUTH
   as she reacts to this. Her head drops. One feels that her last hope has been crushed.

250. CLOSE SHOT   VAN WEYDEN
   as he notices this byplay between Leach and Ruth. For the first time, he becomes aware of their plan.

251. MEDIUM CLOSE   LARSEN AND SAILORS

   > **LARSEN:**
   > *(as he turns back to the men, slowly)*
   > And now gentlemen, do you know what I'm going to do with this list?
   > *(he pauses for effect)*
   > Nothing...absolutely nothing.

   He tears up the paper. Pieces of it whirl around in the wind and flutter across the deck.

252. MEDIUM CLOSE   GROUP
   as the men stare in amazement at this action of Larsen's.

253. CLOSE SHOT   LARSEN[108]
   as righteousness drips from his every word.

   > **LARSEN:**
   > I understand your actions. You felt you had a griev-

ance against me. You felt I was taking advantage of you. Well, you were wrong, gentlemen...I wasn't. What Louie told you the other day was true, every word of it...I have no intention of hunting any seals. I leave that to my brother...he's better equipped for it...
(he pauses, sarcastically)
"Macedonia" is a *modern* boat...it's run by steam. It's got the latest kind of machinery. I can't compete with it. It's the kind of a boat...
(he pauses again, a bitter note coming into his voice)
...that drove most of you off the sea and made you the human wrecks you are...
(his voice becomes sarcastic again)
The "Macedonia" isn't the only one of its kind either. The company that owns it has more...and every year they're building more.
(he looks off at Van Weyden)

253a. CLOSE SHOT   VAN WEYDEN
as he reacts to this.

LARSEN'S VOICE:
(o.s.)
Ten years from now...by 1910 they'll cover the face of the sea...sweeping everything before them...and people like us won't be able to find a vessel like the "Ghost" to ship on...we'll be on the beaches livin' off garbage cans...
(he pauses)

253b. MEDIUM SHOT   LARSEN AND MEN
as he turns to the men.

LARSEN:
Louie forgot to tell you that, didn't he? Sure...sure my brother has cannon on board. Sure...sure he's got them primed to sink the "Ghost." Sure...sure there's a chance of all of you goin' down with this ship, but there's also just as good a chance that you won't.

253c. WIDER ANGLE

as Larsen suddenly walks away from the men and opens the top of a barrel that is standing on deck. He reaches into it and pulls out several seal skins. He looks at them for an instant, then comes back facing the men, holding the skins up in front of the men. He keeps fingering them as he talks.

> LARSEN:
> Each one of these skins is worth money...lots of money. They're soft and smooth and warm. You've got to be rich to be able to afford them. You see, that's the joke. We steal them from the same people that buy them. Certainly, you have no scruples against stealing...

254. REVERSE ANGLE   SHOOTING PAST LARSEN TOWARDS MEN

> LARSEN:
> *(a grin spreading over his face)*
> ...if you get your share of the loot.

The tension is completely broken. The men grin sheepishly.

> LARSEN:
> Louie didn't tell you that either, did he? Well, you will get your share. I promise you that...
> *(quickly)*
> If this voyage turns out well, you'll each have enough to keep you for the rest of your lives.

A mutter of approval goes up from the men.

> LARSEN:
> And if this voyage doesn't turn out well, you'll die quickly instead of inch by inch...
> *(he shouts off to Van Weyden)*
> Mr. Van Weyden, you'll open up the liquor stores for the men tonight. Give them all they want.

Another roar of approval goes up from the men.

> LARSEN:
> *(he turns to Leach)*
> Mr. Leach...Mr. Johnson...

Both men step forward.

> LARSEN:
> *(his voice takes on an oily quality)*
> You see, there's no reason for you to leave this ship. We're friends now, aren't we?

He extends his hand. Neither of them makes a motion to take it. Larsen smiles, starts to walk back. Suddenly he stops and turns to the men.

> LARSEN:
> Oh yes, gentlemen...there's one more thing I feel I ought to warn you about. You have an informer in your midst.

255. CLOSE SHOT   COOKY
as he reacts sharply, bewildered by this sudden turn of events.

256. MEDIUM CLOSE   LARSEN AND MEN

> LARSEN:
> There's nothing, gentlemen, that I detest more than an informer. As evidence of my good faith, gentlemen, I'll tell you who he is. Cooky gave me this list.

Larsen suddenly turns and walks away.

257. MEDIUM CLOSE   COOKY
as his face twists up in hatred and terror.

> COOKY:
> *(screaming)*
> Ye devil!...ye black 'earted devil!

258. WIDER ANGLE
as the men, glad of this opportunity to let their pent up emo-

tions out on someone, go for Cooky. He tries to make a dash for the hatchway, but he is too late. The men succeed in pinioning him down and carry him struggling and screaming to the stern of the boat. Shouts of "Keel haul him! Teach him a lesson" are HEARD.[109] One of them gets a bow-line, ties it under his arms. The others with a tremendous heave toss him overboard.

259. CLOSE SHOT   COOKY
as he succeeds in grabbing hold of the rail, trying to drag himself back into the boat. Someone hits him over the hands. He disappears from view, screaming as he goes.

260. MEDIUM GROUP SHOT   THE MEN
as they stand at the stern, laughing, shouting like savages. They each take turns in pulling sharply at the rope.

261. CLOSE SHOT   COOKY   IN WATER
as his head appears and disappears from view with each tug.

262. CLOSE SHOT   AT STERN
Suddenly Harrison stops. A terrified look comes over his face. He brushes the men aside.

   HARRISON:
   Shark! Shark astern! Pull him in! Pull him in!

263. THE OCEAN
as a black fin cuts the water, making for Cooky.

264. CLOSE SHOT   COOKY
as he becomes aware of the shark. A horrible scream escapes his lips.

265. STERN
as Larsen rushes down, begins to pull with all his might on the rope, trying to get Cooky in before shark gets him.

266. COOKY
still screaming in the water, grasping desperately at rope, trying

to hoist himself up to it, his legs drawn up as close to his body as he can possibly get them.

267. STERN OF THE BOAT
as the men with one tremendous effort succeed in hoisting Cooky aboard. He falls flat on the deck screaming in anguish.

> **COOKY:**
> My leg! My leg! 'E got my leg!

268. TIGHT GROUP SHOT
as the men look down at the writhing form of Cooky.

> **LARSEN:**
> *(to Van Weyden)*
> Better tie up what's left of his leg before he bleeds to death.

As Van Weyden, a horrified look on his face, bends down

DISSOLVE TO:

272. CLOSE SHOT   SHADOWS OF A GROUP OF MEN   NIGHT[110]
CAMERA PICKS UP the grotesque shadows of men, projected against the bunkhouse wall by the flickering light of the overhead lamp. They are grouped together. O.S. comes the SOUND of their raucous voices raised in a sea shanty, "Whiskey Johnny." CAMERA DRAWS BACK, revealing we are in:

273. INTERIOR   BUNKHOUSE   NIGHT
CAMERA HOLDS on the drunken faces of the men who are singing, then begins to PAN around the room.

274. MEDIUM PANNING SHOT
as CAMERA PICKS UP the inhabitants of the bunkhouse. Some lie sprawled on their bunks, others just sit dully on benches staring into space. All have one thing in common: the fact that the liquor they have consumed has rendered them incapable of any coherent thought. It has served Larsen's purpose well. CAMERA FINALLY COMES TO REST ON:

275. MEDIUM CLOSE SHOT   THE DOOR
as Van Weyden enters. He carries several bottles of liquor in his hand. CAMERA TRUCKS with him as he walks through the room and deposits the bottles on a table. He turns and is about to go back when suddenly o.s. comes the wild, agonized SCREAM of a man who is in tremendous pain. The singing suddenly stops. Again we HEAR the scream. Then . . . a silence.

> A SAILOR:
> *(breaking the silence)*
> That's Cooky.
> *(he yells at the top of his voice)*
> Shut up, Cooky! Shut up! You got no reason to yell. Y'had it comin' to you...y'e had it comin' to you...

The sailor suddenly subsides and sits down at the edge of a bunk, staring dully into space. Van Weyden looks at him. Suddenly Harrison springs up and confronts him.

> HARRISON:
> What are you lookin' at?

Van Weyden doesn't answer and starts to go again. Harrison blocks his way.

> HARRISON:
> You...you don't have much use for us, do you?
> *(pauses)*
> You think Larsen bought us out, don't you? You think we're a lot of drunken swine, don't you?
> *(another pause, then bitterly)*
> Well...you're right. We are...

He pushes Van Weyden out of the door, slamming it shut after him.

276. MEDIUM SHOT   THE CORRIDOR
as Van Weyden walks along it. The singing picks up again, becoming even louder as though the men were trying to drown out the SOUND of Cooky's screaming that still comes in regular

intervals from the storehouse below. Van Weyden reaches the galley door, turns the knob and enters.

277. MEDIUM SHOT   THE GALLEY
as Van Weyden enters. It is completely dark save for the patch of light coming in from the door that Van Weyden has opened. Van Weyden goes to the table and strikes a match, preparatory to lighting the lamp. Suddenly the slam of the door is HEARD behind him. He whirls around. As he does so, an arm comes out of the darkness and grabs him, pulling him over into the sides of the room.

> LEACH'S VOICE:[111]
> *(o.s)*
> If you even breathe hard, you're a dead man.

278. TIGHT TWO SHOT
as Van Weyden identifies Leach in the semi-darkness, his face tense, a dangerous glitter in his eyes. He is holding a knife that he presses to Van Weyden's side.

> LEACH:
> Keep your voice low.
> *(a pause)*
> The key to the supply closet...where is it?

> VAN WEYDEN:
> It's in the pocket of that coat...the one hanging over that bunk.[112]

> LEACH:
> Get it, Johnson.

A figure moves in the darkness and goes over to the bunk.

> LEACH:
> See if it fits...

The figure moves again. The SOUND of a key being fitted into a lock is HEARD, then the creaking SOUND of a door being opened.

JOHNSON:
(his voice pitched low)
It fits.

LEACH:
All right...got the stuff.

Johnson is HEARD moving about in the closet.

VAN WEYDEN:
You're escaping.

LEACH:
No...we're inspecting the galley. We want to see how clean you keep it.

VAN WEYDEN:
Take me with you. If I stay on board this boat any longer, I'll go mad.

LEACH:
(venomously)
You're not gonna stay on board this ship much longer. You're goin' on a trip...a long one.

Van Weyden's eyes open wide. He stares at Leach as though disbelieving what he has heard. Then he looks down at the knife in Leach's hands.

279. WIDER ANGLE
as Johnson suddenly comes into scene.

JOHNSON:
(to Leach)
Put that knife back.

LEACH:
You take care of gettin' the supplies...I'll take care of him.

JOHNSON:[113]
I won't let you kill him, do you hear me?

LEACH:
We can't afford to take the chance of having him shoot his mouth off to Larsen.

> JOHNSON:
> You can trust him.
>
> LEACH:
> On board this ship I wouldn't trust my own mother.

Suddenly the SOUND of footsteps are HEARD. Leach looks around quickly, desperately.

> VAN WEYDEN:
> *(quickly)*
> Get in that closet.
>
> LEACH:
> And be trapped like a rat?...not me.
>
> JOHNSON:
> Get in!!

He shoves Leach ahead of him just as the door opens. The swatch of light throws Van Weyden into bold relief. The two men flatten themselves against the wall. Larsen appears.

> LARSEN:
> Van Weyden...

Van Weyden turns and faces Larsen.

> LARSEN:
> Who's down here with you?

280. TIGHT TWO SHOT   LEACH AND JOHNSON
as they stand in the darkness, flattened against the wall. There is a pause.

> VAN WEYDEN'S VOICE:
> *(o.s)*
> No one...no one's down here with me.
>
> LARSEN'S VOICE:
> *(o.s.)*
> I thought I heard the sound of voices.

> **VAN WEYDEN'S VOICE:**
> You probably heard the men in the foc'sle. They're kind of noisy tonight.

The expression on the two men's faces becomes tenser than ever. There is a long pause.

> **LARSEN'S VOICE:**
> *(there is a tired, strained note in it)*
> Yes...yes...I guess you're right...It must have been the men.

The men relax.

281.   MEDIUM CLOSE   LARSEN AND VAN WEYDEN   AT DOOR
as Larsen turns to go. He suddenly stops.

> **LARSEN:**
> Van Weyden, have you seen my mate? I've been looking all over for him.

Van Weyden shakes his head.

> **LARSEN:**
> *(bitterly)*
> He's probably lying on the deck some place, drunk like the rest of them. Well, I guess I'll have to take the wheel myself.
> *(he starts to go, then stops again, turns quickly and grabs Van Weyden)*
> What was that noise?

> **VAN WEYDEN:**
> What noise?

> **LARSEN:**
> Didn't you hear the sound of a ship's siren in the distance?

> **VAN WEYDEN:**
> I didn't hear any siren. You must be mistaken.

> **LARSEN:**
> You sure you didn't?

Van Weyden nods.

> **LARSEN:**
> Funny...all night I keep hearing the sound of a ship's siren coming closer and closer.

He passes his hand over his head. His face twitches suddenly as a streak of pain sears across his brain. In an instant it is gone. He controls himself.

> **LARSEN:**
> I'll go up on deck.
> *(he walks away)*

282. MEDIUM SHOT　CORRIDOR　SHOOTING FROM VAN WEYDEN'S ANGLE
Van Weyden stands there looking after him. As Larsen walks along the corridor, he staggers a little, almost like a drunken man. As he comes to the bottom step, he walks into it and falls flat on his face. Van Weyden starts forward, but Larsen succeeds in quickly lifting himself to his feet, grasping the hand rail and making his way up the steps. As he disappears from view, Van Weyden quickly turns and goes back into the galley.

283. MEDIUM SHOT　GALLEY
Johnson and Leach have come out of hiding. They stand there as Van Weyden comes down to them.

> **VAN WEYDEN:**
> *(excitement in his voice—he grabs hold of Leach's arm)*
> Now...now's the time for you to escape.

> **JOHNSON:**
> *(amazed)*
> Now?...with him at the wheel?

> **VAN WEYDEN:**
> He won't see you. I tell you, he won't see you.

LEACH:
What're you talkin' about?

VAN WEYDEN:
Don't ask me any questions...Go...go before it's too late!

They both stand there without making a move.

VAN WEYDEN:
(almost enraged at their inability to move)
He can't see...you fools[114]...he's blind!

JOHNSON:
Blind?...

VAN WEYDEN:
Yes. I was with him when he had one of those attacks before. It takes several hours for them to go away. By that time you can be off this boat. You can be safe. Go, I tell you!![115]

Johnson starts to move. Leach stops, faces Van Weyden.

LEACH:
Van Weyden, you could've given us away...you didn't.

VAN WEYDEN:
You're wasting time.

LEACH:[116]
Johnson, you go up on deck. Get the boat ready. I'll go get Ruth.
(he turns to Van Weyden, his gratitude is apparent—suddenly)
Do you still want to go with us?...

DISSOLVE TO:

284. MEDIUM CLOSE GROUP SHOT   AT RAIL
Leach, Van Weyden and Ruth stand at the rail. Johnson is silhouetted against the ship preparing the lifeboat. The noise of the wind and the sea makes it difficult for the voices to carry. Off in the distance at the other side of the boat can be seen the fig-

ure of Larsen at the wheel. It is immobile like a statue. The three of them keep looking at the figure.

285. CLOSE SHOT   LARSEN   AT WHEEL:
He stands there, his fingers gripping the wheel, his eyes staring into space. That he is blind is quite evident.[117]

286. MEDIUM CLOSE   AT RAIL
Ruth keeps staring at Larsen as though fascinated.

> **RUTH:**
> I can't help but feel that he's staring right at us—that he can see us.
>
> **VAN WEYDEN:**
> He can't, I tell you. He can't.
>
> **JOHNSON:**
> *(from the boat)*
> All right. We're ready.
>
> **LEACH:**
> *(to Ruth)*
> Come on.

> **RUTH:**
> *(suddenly)*
> I'm not going!
>
> **LEACH:**
> *(in amazement)*
> What?!

RUTH:

(it is evident that the events of the night have proven too much for her. She is in a state of hysteria)
No...I'm not going. You go without me. I'm a jinx. Everything I've ever touched...everything I've ever done has turned out wrong. You'll never make it with me on board. Something'll happen.

LEACH:
(fiercely)
You getting in that boat?

RUTH:
No...no...go without me, I tell you...go without me.

Leach, suddenly and desperately hits her on the jaw and catches her before she slumps to the deck. He turns to Van Weyden.

LEACH:
Gimme a hand...

The two men lift her into the boat. Johnson begins to lower the ropes of the cables. The block and tackle make a creaking noise. The boat disappears from view, as we HEAR the SOUNDS of the seamen singing their chanty which has never stopped during the course of the entire scene. Intermingled with the singing, just as the scene is about to DISSOLVE, we hear Cooky's screams again.

DISSOLVE TO:

287. LONG SHOT   THE BOAT   DAWN
as she appears, under her small sail, out of the early morning mist.

DISSOLVE THRU TO:

288. INTERIOR BOAT   MEDIUM SHOT
Curled up in the forward part of the boat is Ruth, apparently fast asleep. Next to her sits Leach. His head is buried on his chest, giving one the feeling he has suddenly dropped off to

sleep. In the center of the boat is Van Weyden. At the tiller is Johnson.

289. MEDIUM CLOSE   LEACH
as he suddenly awakens, rubs his eyes, looks up at the morning sky, looks over at Johnson standing at the helm. Shaking the sleep once more out of his eyes, Leach starts to make his way quietly toward Johnson. CAMERA MOVES with him as:

290. MEDIUM CLOSE   TRUCKING SHOT
as Leach makes his way toward the forward part of the boat. He passes Van Weyden who awakens also.

291. MEDIUM SHOT   AT STERN
as Leach approaches Johnson.

> **LEACH:**
> *(eagerly)*
> How far have we gone?
>
> **JOHNSON:**
> *(smiling at his eagerness)*
> Not very far. We've only been sailing about six hours. We have a long way to go yet, but with a good wind...and luck...
> *(he pauses)*
> we'll make it.

Van Weyden enters scene.

> **LEACH:**
> I'll go fix some grub....
> *(he moves in direction of Ruth)*
> She'll be up soon.

CAMERA MOVES with him as he bends down.

292. CLOSE SHOT   LEACH
as he starts getting the food. Suddenly into his eyes comes a look of surprise. Tied to the water keg is a string with a note on

it. He tears the note off and reads it. His face blackens with anger. He crumples the note in his hand.

293. WIDER ANGLE
as Van Weyden and Johnson, noticing this, bend down and come over next to him. He turns to them, then hands Van Weyden the note. Van Weyden smoothes it out and reads it, with Johnson looking over his shoulder.

294. INSERT   THE CRUMPLED NOTE
It reads:

Pleasant Journey!
Wolf Larsen

295. CLOSE GROUP SHOT
The three men sit there for an instant as though stunned. Suddenly Leach springs into action. He uncorks the keg and takes a swig from it. No sooner does he taste it, than he makes a wry face and spits it out. With a sudden, angry heave, he hurls the keg into the ocean. It makes a loud SPLASH.

296. CLOSE SHOT   RUTH
as she suddenly awakens. She looks over at the men, notices the tense, worried expressions on their faces, and starts to go towards them.

297. WIDER ANGLE   THE GROUP
as Ruth approaches. She turns and looks at the men. Van Wey-

den hands her the note. She reads it, then slowly turns and looks at Leach.

> **LEACH:**
> He filled the water keg with vinegar...I guess there's no use tryin' the others.
>
> **VAN WEYDEN:**
> *(hopefully)*
> We've still got the keg we took with us last night.
>
> **LEACH:**
> *(bitterly)*
> Two gallons of water...fifteen hundred miles to go.
>
> **JOHNSON:**
> If we manage it well...
>
> **LEACH:**
> *(repeating)*
> Two gallons of water...fifteen hundred miles to go... four people...
>
> **RUTH:**
> *(repeating after him)*
> Four people....
>
> **JOHNSON:**
> I tell you, if we manage it well...
>
> **LEACH:**
> *(fiercely, suddenly grabbing him)*
> And I tell you we will...
> *(he turns off, shakes his fist at the ocean. His anger and bitterness are so great he is almost sobbing)*
> So you think you tricked us, don't you? Sure, I can see you now, sittin' on that deck and laughin' at us... but that laugh'll choke in your throat, because we'll make it...we'll make it...water or no water...
> *(he shouts at the top of his voice)*
> D'ye hear me, Larsen?...We'll make it!!

There is a silence, broken only by the noise of the ocean. The group stands huddled in their despair, in the stern of the boat as we

DISSOLVE TO:

297a. CLOSE SHOT   LARSEN   ON BRIDGE   MORNING
He stands there etched against the sky, staring straight ahead of him. Across the scene comes a few stray wisps of fog that seem to blow in from the starboard side of the boat. The SOUND of running footsteps is HEARD. Larsen doesn't turn his head but keeps staring straight ahead.

297b. WIDER ANGLE
as Smoke, the hunter, comes running up to Larsen.

> **SMOKE:**
> *(excitement in his voice)*
> Captain Larsen...the number two dory...it's missing!
>
> **LARSEN:**
> *(slowly)*
> I know.
>
> **SMOKE:**
> Leach...Johnson...the girl...Van Weyden...
>
> **LARSEN:**
> *(abruptly)*
> I know that too.
>
> **SMOKE:**
> They couldn't have gotten very far. We can still head them off!
>
> **LARSEN:**
> There's no hurry. We'll pick them up...in a few days.

Smoke looks at him strangely. Suddenly o.s. the SOUND of a dull boom is HEARD in the distance. Smoke turns and looks off.

297c. LONG SHOT   THE HORIZON   (MINIATURE)
Far in the distance can be seen the smoke stacks of a steamer.

A puff of smoke that has accompanied the shot still hangs in the air.

297d. MEDIUM CLOSE   THE BRIDGE
as the SOUND of a splash is HEARD o.s.

> SMOKE:
> *(the tension of the moment is reflected in his eyes)*
> It's a steamer!
> *(he looks off again)*
> It looks like...
>
> LARSEN:
> *(without looking off)*
> It's my brother's ship, the "Macedonia." He's caught up to me.

Another boom is HEARD. A silence, then again the SPLASH of water as the shell hits the boat.

297e.   MEDIUM SHOT   MAIN DECK
as the crew comes streaming on board, their fright apparent on each of their faces.

297f.   MEDIUM CLOSE   THE BRIDGE   LARSEN AND SMOKE

> SMOKE:
> *(anxiously)*
> What orders, sir?[118]

142   *The Sea Wolf*

> **LARSEN:**
> *(he shakes his head as though trying to clear it)*
> Orders?...

Another shot is HEARD.

> **SMOKE:**
> They're coming closer. They'll soon catch up to us. We might give him the slip if we make for that fog bank...
>
> **LARSEN:**
> Fog bank?
>
> **SMOKE:**
> *(impatiently)*
> Yes...there's one ahead of us about a mile off the port side...

297g. LONG SHOT   THE HORIZON   (MINIATURE)
as we see the low hanging fog bank Smoke speaks about.

297h. MEDIUM PANNING SHOT   THE DECK   THE CREW
as the CAMERA PICKS UP their faces, looking up at Larsen. On each face is the same panic, the same question.

297i. MEDIUM CLOSE   THE BRIDGE   LARSEN AND SMOKE

> **SMOKE:**
> *(anxiously)*
> Can't you see it?

Larsen turns his head and looks off.

297j. LONG SHOT   THE HORIZON   (MINIATURE)
We see the ocean now through Larsen's eyes . . . murky, hazy, indistinct . . . the way a man who has lost most of his vision would see it.

297k. MEDIUM CLOSE   THE BRIDGE

LARSEN:
(as he turns back to Smoke)[119]
Yes...yes, the fog...I see it. Take the wheel, Smoke. Make for the fog bank.[120]

He walks away from the wheel. Smoke looks at him completely bewildered as we

DISSOLVE THRU TO:

297l. LONG SHOT   THE "GHOST"
as she disappears into the fog bank. We hold on the fog for an instant, then

DISSOLVE THRU TO:

297m. MEDIUM SHOT   THE DECK   FOG
There is not a sound on board, save for the creaking of the ship. Dim figures wrapped in the fog are outlined at various parts of the boat. The men . . . each one at his post . . . standing stock still . . . like carved shadows.

297n. MEDIUM CLOSE   COOKY
He lies sprawled on a coil of ropes. On his face is still the pain of his missing leg. In his eyes is the hatred he feels for Larsen. Next to him lies a pair of improvised crutches. The tread of a man's heavy boots are HEARD on the deck. He looks up.

297o. WIDER ANGLE
as Larsen approaches. His figure looms ever larger and more ominous in the fog. He walks slowly and with great deliberation. In the darkness he almost stumbles over Cooky. He quickly regains his balance.

COOKY:
(his voice filled with hatred)
I'm sorry, sir...there's no place else for me to be. I'm afraid to be below deck, sir...if we start to sink, sir...

LARSEN:
Shut up!!
(he stares down at Cooky as though he saw him)
We're not gonna sink.

COOKY:
(his voice saccharine)
I'm sure we're not, sir. I'm sure you'll pull us through, sir.

LARSEN:
(viciously)
And if that twisted brain of yours has any schemes in it...like cryin' out and givin' away our position...

COOKY:
(whining)
Not me, sir...I wouldn't do a thing like that, sir.

LARSEN:
If you do, there's a bullet in Smoke's gun with your name written on it.

Suddenly o.s. is HEARD the roar of the "Macedonia's" gun. This time it is much closer. There is a great roar and then a loud crashing, splintering noise.

SMOKE:
(suddenly to Larsen)
Look out!!
(he pushes him out of the way)

297p. CLOSE SHOT   THE MAIN TOPSAIL
as it hangs perilously to the mainmast and then goes crashing to the deck below.

297q. MEDIUM SHOT   THE DECK
as it lands. The men scurry out of the way. There is a long pause. The men stand tense, each looking at the other, the fear of their impending fate reflected in their eyes. The hunters grip their rifles tighter and face the men. Suddenly the young boy drops to his knees and begins to sob.

LARSEN:
(walking towards him)
Shut him up.

HARRISON
(quickly)
He's very young, sir. He ran away to sea. He didn't think it would be like this...he's frightened.

LARSEN:
Make him shut up!

Another shot is HEARD . . . another crash. Some more debris falls on deck.

SMOKE:
They must have sighted us, sir.
(he points off)

LARSEN:
No...they haven't. They're just shooting blind. We'll lose them in another minute...

HARRISON:
(suddenly)
The "Macedonia"...I see her!

LARSEN:
Where?...where?

HARRISON:
(pointing excitedly)
There...through the fog.

Larsen, bewildered not knowing where he means, turns the other way. Harrison doesn't notice this.

HARRISON:
Do you see her, sir?

LARSEN:
(trying to keep up his bluff)
Yes...yes...I see her.

297r. CLOSE SHOT   COOKY
as he reacts to this. His eyes open wide, as though he can't believe what he has seen.

297s. MEDIUM CLOSE   DECK
as Harrison turns around and notices Larsen looking the other way.

> **HARRISON:**
> On the port side, sir.
>
> **LARSEN:**
> *(quickly)*
> Yes...I know. I wanted to see how near we were to the other side of the fog bank...
> *(he turns and looks off)*

297t. LONG SHOT   THE FOG SHROUDED OCEAN   (MINIATURE)
Dimly through the fog, we see the smoke stacks and the rigging of the "Macedonia." From it comes another blinding flash and a roar.

297u. MEDIUM CLOSE   THE DECK
as a loud, splintering crash is HEARD below.

> **SMOKE:**
> I think that one got us, sir...Shall I order the life boats lowered?
>
> **LARSEN:**
> *(firmly)*
> No!! No man leaves this ship until I give the word. We've still got a chance as long as we're afloat.

297v. MEDIUM PANNING SHOT   THE CREW
as they react to this. It is a choice between their fear of drowning and the fear of the guns trained on them by the hunters. Larsen starts walking away from them.

297w. CLOSE SHOT   COOKY
He watches as Larsen walks away from the crew and toward

him. A cunning look comes into his eyes. He laboriously crawls out of the coil of ropes on which he has been lying and makes his way along the deck.

297x. WIDER ANGLE
as Larsen approaches him, looking straight ahead of him. Cooky, with a last desperate effort, manages to get in front of him. Larsen, who is unable to see, stumbles over him and falls on all fours to the deck. CAMERA MOVES INTO A:

297y. CLOSE SHOT   COOKY
as over his face comes a look of wild triumph.

> **COOKY:**
> *(shouting out savagely)*
> 'E's blind!—'e's blind!

297z. MEDIUM SHOT   THE CREW
as they turn and react to this.

297aa. CLOSE SHOT   LARSEN
on all fours on the deck, for the first time fear showing in his face. O.S. comes Cooky's voice, carrying with it all the implications of this discovery.

> **COOKY'S VOICE:**
> 'E's blind, I tell ye...the beggar's blind!!

We stay on Larsen's tensed face as o.s. comes the SOUND of the approaching men's feet and another CRASH from the "Macedonia's" cannon.

DISSOLVE THRU TO:

298. THE SKY[121]   DAY
It is high noon and the sun is directly overhead, beating down with all its intensity on the ocean.

299. LONG SHOT   THE DORY
There is very little wind. The sails hang loosely from the masts. The boat seems to be crawling through the water.

300. MEDIUM CLOSE   INTERIOR BOAT
They all sit there, helplessly waiting for the wind to come, the perspiration on their faces indicating the intense heat.

> **JOHNSON:**
> *(to Van Weyden)*
> Mr. Van Weyden...it's high noon...You'll ration the water.

Van Weyden gets up and very carefully and slowly pours out the water for each of them. He passes it around. They all drink slowly as though it were rare wine. There is a dead pause.

> **JOHNSON:**
> *(trying to be casual)*
> You see...if you manage well...

> **RUTH:**
> *(suddenly turning on Leach, savagely. She is cracking up)*
> I told you what would happen, didn't I? You wouldn't listen to me...I begged you not to take me...

Leach suddenly grabs her arms and holds them tight against her sides.

> **LEACH:**
> *(his voice low)*
> Quiet, Ruth...quiet. We'll make it...
> *(he turns to the others)*
> Won't we?

There is a silence.

> **LEACH:**
> *(fiercely)*
> Tell her we'll make it!

> **JOHNSON:**
> *(nodding his head slowly)*
> Sure...sure...

Van Weyden turns his face away, as we

DISSOLVE TO:

301. LONG SHOT   THE BOAT   NIGHT
The wind has come back and whipped up the waves. The boat appears and disappears in the giant swells.

302. INTERIOR BOAT
Johnson is at the helm. Leach and Van Weyden are up forward working on the sail. The boat veers sharply.

> **JOHNSON:**
> No! Not that way...wait a minute. I'll show you.
> *(he turns to Ruth who has been sitting next to him)*
> You hold onto the helm. Just keep her as she is.

He starts to go forward. As he does so:

303. CLOSE SHOT   RUTH
at the helm. As she sits there, suddenly into her eyes comes a wild look. She gets up quickly, lets go of the helm and starts to climb on top of the seat as though she were about to jump off. As she does, the boat swerves sharply.

304. THE MEN   IN THE FORWARD PART OF THE BOAT
The sudden swerve of the boat causes them to grasp desperately onto the mast for support. Suddenly into Leach's eyes comes a look of horror.

> **LEACH:**
> *(shouting)*
> Ruth! No! No!

He makes a mad dash for the stern.

305. MEDIUM CLOSE   STERN
as Leach succeeds in reaching Ruth. He grabs her arm and then almost ferociously hurls her into the center of the boat. She lies there for an instant as though stunned. Then as she is about to

get up, Leach comes over to her quickly and pinions her arms close to her sides, holding her tightly against the seat. His face is drawn and white with both anger and terror at what she was about to do. There is a long pause.

306. WIDER ANGLE
as Van Weyden and Johnson come into scene. Johnson looks at them for an instant, then goes back to grab the tiller and try to straighten out the course of the boat which is now careening wildly in the mounting sea. Van Weyden stays in the center of the boat, looking down at both Leach and Ruth.

307. MEDIUM CLOSE   LEACH AND RUTH
After a while Leach calms down to be able to speak.

> **LEACH:**
> I'll tie you to the mast with a rope.
> *(Ruth is silent)*
> D'ye hear me?

> **RUTH:**
> *(slowly)*
> I hear you.

> **LEACH:**
> You gotta swear to me you won't try anything like that again.
> *(again she is silent)*
> Will you swear?

There is a long pause.

> **RUTH:**
> No.

> **LEACH:**
> *(his voice tortured)*
> Ruth! Ruth!

> **RUTH:**
> Listen to me...

LEACH:
(angrily)
I don't wanna listen to you.

RUTH:
(continuing)
If you three make it...

LEACH:
Four...say four...

308. CLOSE SHOT   JOHNSON AT HELM
as he reacts to the scene.

LEACH'S VOICE:
(o.s.)
Either we all make it...or none of us do.

309. TIGHT TWO SHOT   RUTH AND LEACH

RUTH:
Mr. Van Weyden...Mr. Johnson...they got somethin' to look forward to...You, too...you can still make a new life for yourself some place.

LEACH:
You?...how about you?

RUTH:
(turning on him, fiercely)
Do you really want me to tell you?

LEACH:
(as fiercely)
Yeah...yeah!!

RUTH:
(her voice tortured)
All right...here it is. We'll make land. Maybe I'll get to Singapore...or to Hong Kong...I've been there before. I know how to get around. All right. Nobody'll spot me. I won't have to go back to jail...
(her voice rises)

>   How do you think I'll get along?...How do you think I'll live?...
>
>   **LEACH:**
>   *(in a blind rage)*
>   Shut up!!

There is a pause.

>   **RUTH:**
>   *(her voice small)*
>   You asked me to tell you.
>
>   **LEACH:**
>   Now I'll tell you! When we get to land...if we get there ...I'll make a livin' for you. You'll stay with me.
>   *(she looks at him sharply)*
>   We'll be married...
>
>   **RUTH:**
>   *(quickly)*
>   What?
>
>   **LEACH:**
>   I said we'd be married.

There is a long pause. Ruth looks at him, seeming to disbelieve what she has heard, then she turns and looks off.

310.   WIDER ANGLE
as she turns to Van Weyden.

>   **RUTH:**
>   *(to Van Weyden)*
>   Don't let him talk like that...don't let him make it tougher for me...don't let him lie to me.
>
>   **VAN WEYDEN:**
>   *(slowly)*
>   I don't think he's lying, Ruth.

RUTH:
(turning to Leach)
You must be crazy...

LEACH:
Yeah...that's right—I'm crazy—with lovin' you—

RUTH:
(incredulously)
Lovin' me?...
(she turns again to Van Weyden)
You'll see...he'll forget he ever said those things...he's sayin' them now because...because...

Her voice trails off. She turns and looks at Leach, pitifully, as though she wants to deny what she is going to say.

RUTH:
He's sorry for me.

LEACH:
I ought to break your neck for sayin' that.

There is a pause.

LEACH:
We'll be married...like I said.

RUTH:
(pleading)
Do you know what I've been? Do you know what I've done?

LEACH:
(angrily)
Do you know what *I've* been?...do you know what *I've* done?
(he grabs her arm)

311. TIGHT TWO SHOT   LEACH AND RUTH
as Leach holds her close to him.

LEACH:
What's done is done...it's over with. We can start a new life...both of us...unless...

RUTH:
(quickly)
Unless what?

LEACH:
(slowly)
Unless you don't wanna...unless the kind of life you've lived has been part of you...unless that's the way you wanna go on livin'.

RUTH:
(earnestly)
No...no...I don't. I don't...I swear I don't.

LEACH:
All right...neither do I. We'll start off from scratch. There's a spot for us someplace in the world...we'll find it.

There is a pause.

RUTH:
(shaking her head)
If I could only believe that...
(pleading)
Make me believe it!!

LEACH:
(holding her closer)
Ruth...listen...what I'm gettin' at...what I'm tryin' to say...is...
(he beats his fist against the boat in sheer desperation at his loss of words. Suddenly he turns to Van Weyden)
You...you...you know how to use words...
(he pleads)
Talk to her for me.

DISSOLVE TO:

A Screenplay 155

312. MEDIUM SHOT   THE OCEAN   NIGHT
as the boat comes out of the darkness and appears in a swath of silver light thrown upon the ocean by the moon.

> DISSOLVE THROUGH TO:

313. CLOSE SHOT   INTERIOR BOAT   PROW
Both Ruth and Leach are fast asleep, she curled up against him. On their faces is still reflected the tense struggle they have gone through earlier in the night. CAMERA DRAWS BACK TO INCLUDE:

314. CLOSE SHOT   VAN WEYDEN
as he sits in the center of the boat, his eyes focused upon them. Suddenly he turns and looks back over his shoulder to:

315. CLOSE SHOT   JOHNSON
as he sits at the helm, his face as impassive as ever.

316. WIDER ANGLE   STERN
as Van Weyden approaches Johnson and sits directly opposite him. Johnson keeps his eyes fixed on the ocean ahead as though he were not aware of Van Weyden's presence. There is a longer pause. Van Weyden moves closer to him.

317. MEDIUM CLOSE   VAN WEYDEN AND JOHNSON
In Van Weyden's eyes is a troubled look.

> **VAN WEYDEN:**
> There's not much chance, is there, Mr. Johnson?
>
> **JOHNSON:**
> *(he is evidently avoiding Van Weyden's question)*
> There's a good wind tonight...
>
> **VAN WEYDEN:**
> *(eagerly)*
> Perhaps a passing ship—
>
> **JOHNSON:**
> Perhaps.
> *(for the first time he takes his eyes off the ocean and turns to*

Van Weyden)
You know how to read a chart, Mr. Van Weyden?

VAN WEYDEN:
Yes.
(he looks at Johnson trying to make out what he is trying to get at)
Why?

JOHNSON:
(noncommittally)
One can never tell. Something might happen to...
(he pauses)
...anyone of us.
(suddenly)
How old are you, Mr. Van Weyden?

VAN WEYDEN:
Thirty-five.

JOHNSON:
(he speaks strangely)
I am almost sixty.
(he looks off)
Van Weyden follows his gaze.

318. MEDIUM CLOSE   PROW
Ruth and Leach, the moon lighting up their faces, are still asleep.

319. MEDIUM CLOSE   JOHNSON AND VAN WEYDEN
as Van Weyden turns quickly to Johnson.

VAN WEYDEN:
(as the idea of what Johnson is getting at seeps into his mind)
Mr. Johnson...!

JOHNSON:
Yes, Mr. Van Weyden...

VAN WEYDEN:
Something will happen...I know it will...we'll sight a boat.

JOHNSON:
Perhaps.

VAN WEYDEN:
You're tired. I'll take the helm.

JOHNSON:
No...no...It is a good feeling to be able to sail a boat for myself for a change...instead of for someone else.
(he fingers the tiller lovingly)
Many times when I was at the wheel of the "Ghost," I used to imagine that it was my ship...
(he sighs)
The "Ghost" is a beautiful ship...
(his face lights up as he talks)
Her sails are like the wings of a gull. She answers to the touch of your hand at the wheel like a high-strung horse to the touch of the bit...the ropes hum in tune like the strings of a violin...
(passionately)
I would give my life to own a vessel like the "Ghost."

VAN WEYDEN:
Maybe you will one day.

JOHNSON:
Maybe...

There is a pause. Johnson speaks softly.

JOHNSON:
Goodnight, Mr. Van Weyden.

VAN WEYDEN:
Goodnight, Mr. Johnson.

Van Weyden starts to go back toward the center of the boat as we

DISSOLVE TO:

320. to 324. OMITTED[122]

325. LONG SHOT   THE OCEAN   FOG
as dawn breaks over it.

> DISSOLVE THRU TO

326. MEDIUM CLOSE   THE PROW OF THE BOAT   FOG
as Leach awakens. He gently withdraws his arm from Ruth so as not to awaken her. Then he starts to go toward the stern of the boat. Suddenly he stops short. A look of amazement comes into his eyes, then one of horror.

> **LEACH:**
> Johnson! Johnson!

327. MEDIUM CLOSE   VAN WEYDEN   FOG
as he awakens with a start. Off scene comes:

> **LEACH'S VOICE:**
> Johnson!!

He looks sharply toward the stern.

328. CLOSE SHOT   THE STERN   FOG
It is empty. The tiller has been lashed to the boat by a rope.

> DISSOLVE TO:

329. MEDIUM SHOT   INTERIOR BOAT
The fog is so thick it is difficult to make the three of them out clearly as they sit there listlessly, dully, staring into space. The tiller that Johnson lashed to the boat is still in the same position, indicating the boat is drifting without any human hand guiding it. Not a word is passed. The feeling of bitterness that Johnson's death has caused is apparent on each of their faces. Suddenly Van Weyden starts to walk towards the stores. As he does so, he suddenly stops and looks off. At first he blinks his eyes, disbelieves what he sees. He turns quickly to the others.

VAN WEYDEN:
(his voice hoarse, tense with excitement)
A ship! I see a ship!

They all look off.

330. LONG SHOT   THE HORIZON   (MINIATURE)
as the rigging of a vessel can be seen vaguely through the fog.

DISSOLVE TO:

331. INTERIOR BOAT   (ACTUAL BOAT IN B.G. TO BE SHOT ON STAGE 21)
as Leach tugs desperately at the oars, the sweat pouring down his face. In the b.g. the hull of the vessel looms larger. Van Weyden is at the tiller. Ruth is in front of the boat. The vessel looms still larger and closer on the horizon. Suddenly Van Weyden springs up.

LEACH:
(shouting at him)
Hold her straight...you fool.[123]

VAN WEYDEN:
(slowly)
You can stop rowing, Leach...
(Leach looks at him strangely)
That vessel we're heading for is the "Ghost."

Leach looks at him, then off at horizon. CAMERA MOVES INTO A:

332. CLOSE GROUP SHOT
as the three of them stare off scene, their eyes filled with dull despair.

333. MEDIUM SHOT   THE "GHOST"
as it suddenly looms large in front of them through the fog. For the first time since we have seen the ship, it really lives up to its name: The "Ghost." It just lies there in the water, listing badly

to one side, its mast badly battered. The top of the mainsail looks like it has been chopped down with an axe. It still hangs precariously, the rest of the mast flapping loosely and ominously in the wind. The other sails hang loosely from the gaffs, half of them spilled out over the decks. What little sail remains is torn and ripped.

334. MEDIUM SHOT   INTERIOR BOAT
as the three of them, the astonishment at this sight reflected on their faces, look at each other.

> LEACH:
> *(suddenly)*
> The boats—they're all gone! Look!

335. MEDIUM SHOT
The lines which are used to lower the boats swing idly against the side of the "Ghost." There is a long pause during which the only sound HEARD is the lapping of the water against the "Ghost."

336. MEDIUM CLOSE   INTERIOR BOAT
as Leach suddenly springs to the oars and starts rowing toward the "Ghost."

> RUTH:
> *(suddenly)*
> Where are you going?

> LEACH:
> Aboard the "Ghost." There's water aboard that ship...food...enough to make it a sure thing for us.

> RUTH:
> No...don't...

> LEACH:
> There's nobody on board...can't you see she's sinking...the boats are gone!

> RUTH:
> Larsen?

LEACH:
(viciously)
He probably saved his own skin...first.
(to Van Weyden)
You stay here with her. I'll lower the stuff down to you.

He ties the dory to one of the lines, then springs up and begins to climb up a rope.

337. MEDIUM CLOSE   RUTH AND VAN WEYDEN   SHOOTING UPWARDS
as they watch the figure of Leach climb up, reach the deck, clamber over the rail and then disappear from view. The fear of the unknown is reflected on their faces.

338. MEDIUM SHOT   DECK
as Leach looks about him. He stands at the rail for a moment, tense, his every muscle taut. He listens. There is no sound. The CAMERA MOVES with him as he cautiously starts forward.

339. MEDIUM TRUCKING SHOT   LEACH
as he moves along the fog-shrouded deck. The fog is so thick it is difficult for him to see. As he walks along, we see the deck is a shambles. Everything is broken and shattered. Suddenly he stumbles and falls. He grabs onto something for support. As he does so, a loud, splintering noise is HEARD from above. He looks up quickly.

340. CLOSE SHOT   THE MAST   SHOOTING FROM DECK
The weight of the rigging has caused it to give way a few more feet. It hangs even more perilously than before.

341. CLOSE SHOT   LEACH
as he ducks quickly behind a mast, his knife drawn listening.

342. FULL SHOT   THE DECK
It is empty and silent as before.

343. MEDIUM TRUCKING SHOT   LEACH
as he moves forward, keeping in the shadows, towards the galley.

344. CLOSE SHOT   THE GALLEY DOORS
as Leach approaches. He swings them open, first, then ducks back. There is a long pause. Then Leach, his knife held in his hand, starts to go down the galley. The CAMERA HOLDS on the galley doors as they swing shut behind him.[124]

345. MEDIUM SHOT   INTERIOR BOAT[125]
as Van Weyden and Ruth still stare upwards at the "Ghost."

> **RUTH:**
> *(suddenly)*
> He's been gone a long time.
>
> **VAN WEYDEN:**
> Only a few minutes.
>
> **RUTH:**
> It seems like hours.

There is a pause.

> **VAN WEYDEN:**
> He'll be back.

Suddenly she springs to her feet.

> **RUTH:**
> *(shouting)*
> George! George!!

346. MEDIUM SHOT   THE "GHOST"
as she lies in the water. The only SOUND one HEARS is the echo of Ruth's voice.

347. MEDIUM SHOT   INTERIOR BOAT
as Ruth stares at Van Weyden, her eyes filled with horror at the silence. She shouts again.

> **RUTH:**
> George! George!!

Again the silence, again the echo. She turns to Van Weyden. There is an imploring look on her face.

> **VAN WEYDEN:**
> *(slowly)*
> We'd better go up and look for him.

He starts for the rope.

DISSOLVE TO:

348. MEDIUM SHOT   MAIN DECK   THE "GHOST"
as Van Weyden helps Ruth on board. They, too, stand there for a moment, surveying the wreckage. Then they start moving toward the galley.

349. MEDIUM CLOSE   THE GALLEY
as Van Weyden tries to open the door. He pushes on it. The doors swing open—both enter.

349a. MEDIUM CLOSE   CORRIDOR
as Ruth and Van Weyden descend the steps and go into the corridor leading to the foc'sle. It is deathly quiet, save for the creaking of the ship.

> **VAN WEYDEN:**
> *(a soft, yet penetrating voice)*
> Leach! Leach! Where are you? Leach! Where are you?

Suddenly o.s. is HEARD a muffled noise as though someone were knocking on the door. The CAMERA MOVES with them as they walk towards the storeroom door. It is a heavy iron door with a padlock on it.

349b. TIGHT TWO SHOT   RUTH AND VAN WEYDEN   AT DOOR

> **LEACH'S VOICE:**
> *(faintly, through the door)*
> Here! I'm here! Can you hear me?

VAN WEYDEN:
Yes...we can hear you.

LEACH'S VOICE:
All right...then listen...

VAN WEYDEN:
There's no time for words now...

349c. MEDIUM CLOSE   INTERIOR STOREROOM   LEACH
The room is almost pitch dark. His face is just dimly outlined.

LEACH:
(his voice taut)
Listen to me! There isn't a chance in the world of breaking this door down in time...

VAN WEYDEN'S VOICE:
We'll find a way...

LEACH:
(disregarding him)
There's a lot of stuff I've got piled up outside the galley...water...food...I had it all ready when Larsen came behind me. I didn't even a chance to holler...get that stuff...put it on board the dory...quick...

RUTH'S VOICE:
And you? How about you?

LEACH:
Don't stand there wasting time. Get off the boat before he gets you too...get off it, I say!

349d. MEDIUM CLOSE   INTERIOR CORRIDOR RUTH   AND VAN WEYDEN
as they stand huddled at the doorway. They speak in whispers.

RUTH:
The ship is sinking...You'll drown...

LEACH'S VOICE:
All right...I'll drown...my number's up. I knew it was up the minute I first came on board.

RUTH:
(desperately)
There's got to be a way to get you out of here...there's got to...

LEACH'S VOICE:
Sure...sure...there's a way. Larsen's got the key. All you gotta do is ask him for it.

RUTH:
(desperately)
I'll get it from him.

349e. CLOSE SHOT   INTERIOR STOREROOM   LEACH
His face is white with the tension.

LEACH:
(pleading)
Stay away from him. He's not only blind...he's mad...If you ever get near those hands of his, he'll tear you to pieces...you've gotta live...

349f. MEDIUM CLOSE   RUTH AND VAN WEYDEN   INTERIOR CORRIDOR

RUTH:
Not without you!

LEACH'S VOICE:
Van Weyden...make her go with you.

RUTH:[126]
The only part of my life that's ever meant anything to me is the few days I've known you.

VAN WEYDEN:
Ruth...maybe...

RUTH:
No...no, there's no maybe about it...without him. There's no life for me. He said it himself...you heard him say it in the boat last night.

There is a pause.

VAN WEYDEN:
(as he looks at her tortured face)
Stay here.
(his face becomes hard)
I'll get the key from Larsen.

Suddenly he walks away.

349g. CLOSE SHOT   LEACH
as he hears Van Weyden's retreating footsteps.

LEACH:
Van Weyden...Van Weyden!
(he shouts in desperation)
Come back...Come back, do you hear me? Take her with you...get off this boat...Van Weyden!!

The footsteps die away. There is a long period of silence. He shrugs his shoulders like a man resigned to his fate. He moves closer to the door.

LEACH:
(his voice soft)
Ruth...Ruth...you still there?

349h. CLOSE SHOT   RUTH   INTERIOR CORRIDOR
as she stands huddled against the door.

RUTH:
Yes...I'm still here.

LEACH'S VOICE:
You shouldn't have stayed...you shouldn't have stayed.

RUTH:
(simply)
If you live...I live...If you die...I die. That's the way it is with me...

349i. CLOSE SHOT   LEACH   INTERIOR STOREROOM
After a long pause:

LEACH:
(sadly)
Funny how your sayin' that makes me think of one thing. I once went to a weddin' of a friend of mine ...the one part of it that stuck in my mind was when they both repeated after the priest...
(he thinks for a moment)
For better or for worse, for richer or for poorer, in sickness and in health, to love and to cherish...*till death do us part.*
(another pause)
I guess we're gonna skip everything but the last part...

350. CLOSE SHOT   RUTH   INTERIOR CORRIDOR
Her face takes on a strange smile.

RUTH:[127]
No...that's not true. We've had all the rest. It just happened quicker with us, that's all. We crowded all of our life together into a few days. I never even expected that much...
(she chokes up for an instant, then regains control)
So if this is the way it's gotta end, it's all right with me.

There is a pause.

> **LEACH'S VOICE:**
> *(softly)*
> With me, too.

351. **MEDIUM CLOSE   STAIRWAY LEADING TO OFFICERS' QUARTERS**
    As Van Weyden appears. He looks about the officers' mess. It too is a shambles, the tables overturned, the curtain ripped from the windows. He looks about him for an instant, then looks towards Larsen's cabin. Slowly he approaches it. He tries the knob. As he slowly turns it, Larsen's voice is HEARD o.s.:

    > **LARSEN'S VOICE:**
    > Come in, Van Weyden...the door is open.

    Van Weyden hesitates for an instant, then slowly he opens the door.

352. **MEDIUM SHOT   LARSEN'S CABIN**
    as Van Weyden approaches. Larsen sits there in a chair facing the door, staring straight ahead of him. There is a long pause as the two men face each other. Van Weyden stands framed in the doorway, the open door at his back.

    > **LARSEN:**
    > *(after a pause)*
    > I was expecting you.
    >
    > **VAN WEYDEN:**
    > *(tensely)*
    > The key to the storeroom. I want it.
    >
    > **LARSEN:**
    > *(softly)*
    > Come and take it from me, Mr. Van Weyden.

    Van Weyden moves toward him. As he does so, a gun suddenly appears in Larsen's hand.

    > **LARSEN:**
    > If you take another step...I'll blow your brains out...[128]

353. CLOSE SHOT   VAN WEYDEN
We see Van Weyden through Larsen's eyes, blurred, vague, and distorted. Every time we see Van Weyden in this scene in a separate shot, we see him that way.

354. REVERSE ANGLE   SHOOTING PAST VAN WEYDEN
There is another pause.

> LARSEN:
> *(suddenly)*
> Where's Johnson? Why didn't he come on board with you?[129]
>
> VAN WEYDEN:
> *(slowly)*
> Johnson's dead. He gave up his life...
>
> LARSEN:
> I'm disappointed. I thought it would be you who would make the noble sacrifice.
> *(taunting)*
> Why didn't you, Mr. Van Weyden?
>
> VAN WEYDEN:
> This ship is sinking...there's not much time.
>
> LARSEN:
> *(slowly)*
> I've got all the time in the world. Answer me, Mr. Van Weyden, why didn't you?

Van Weyden moves toward him. Larsen points the gun at him.

355. CLOSE SHOT   LARSEN
as a grin spreads over his face. The expression in his eyes leaves no doubt but that he is slightly insane.

> LARSEN:
> All your fine words, Mr. Van Weyden, were just fine words, weren't they? I was right all the time, wasn't I? When you were faced with the choice yourself, you let Johnson die.[130] Once you said to me that "there's a

price no man will pay for living"...what's your price, Van Weyden?

356. MEDIUM CLOSE   VAN WEYDEN AND LARSEN
It is evident Van Weyden is still trying to reason with him.

VAN WEYDEN:
You can go along with us in the boat. When we reach shore, I'll get you a doctor. He'll fix your eyes for you. You'll be able to see again.

LARSEN:
Thank you, Mr. Van Weyden, but I'll never be able to see again. I know that...I've known it for a long time. This is the finish...for my eyes...for myself...I sink with my ship. That should appeal to you, Mr. Van Weyden...
(bitterly)
It's in the best literary tradition of the sea.
(he pauses)
I, Wolf Larsen, sink with my own ship...*in sight of land*!

VAN WEYDEN:
(astounded)
Land?

LARSEN:
Yes...land...we're lying two miles off an island.

VAN WEYDEN:
I don't believe you.

357. MEDIUM SHOT   VAN WEYDEN AND LARSEN

LARSEN:
It's right beyond the fog bank. You'll see it when the fog lifts.
(he continues)
It's not much of an island. A few Japanese fishing boats put in there once in a while...that's where I was heading for before my brother caught up to me...
(another pause)

That's the kind of island your friends...Leach...and the
girl...dreamed about, isn't it?

VAN WEYDEN:
Yes...that's the kind of island they dreamed about.

LARSEN:
(mocking)
Too bad Leach didn't know about it.

Suddenly the boat lists sharply. Van Weyden clutches onto the
door to maintain his footing. Some water begins to seep into
the room.

LARSEN:[131]
She's settling fast, Mr. Van Weyden...You'd better go.

VAN WEYDEN:
Go?

LARSEN:
Yes...you can go...I won't stop you...take the girl with
you, too.

There is a pause.

LARSEN:
(his mad ego becoming apparent)
I want you to finish writing that book about me...the
last chapter should be a good one. Too bad you
weren't on board when it all happened. It was excit-

ing. From the first moment that my brother's boat sighted us...we made a run for it...

Van Weyden makes another move towards him.

> **LARSEN:**
> I saw you move!

Van Weyden stops.

> **LARSEN:**
> *(he continues his story)*
> We slipped into this fog bank. For a full hour I bluffed the crew. Nobody on board knew I was blind. Then Cooky...Cooky found out. " 'E's blind!"...he yelled. "The beggar's blind"...
> *(he laughs)*
> He called *me...me*....a beggar!
> *(he pauses)*
> Then my brother fired pointblank at us. The "Ghost" began to sink. They ran for the boats...like rats they ran...
> *(again he laughs)*
> I had a pair of crutches made for Cooky. The last thing he did was hit me with them. That was Cooky's greatest moment. If they hadn't been in such a hurry to get off, I guess they would have let him kill me. That would have been a wonderful end for Wolf Larsen, wouldn't it?...to be beaten to death by Cooky's crutches...You'll write all of this in your book, won't you?

The boat lists sharply again.

> **LARSEN:**
> You'd better hurry.
>
> **VAN WEYDEN:**
> Leach?...what about Leach?

LARSEN:
(his face hard)
He goes down with me.

VAN WEYDEN:[132]
Why? Why?

LARSEN:
He set the crew against me...he once tried to kill me.

VAN WEYDEN:
(bitterly)
And this is your revenge.

LARSEN:
Yeah...yeah...this is my revenge.

VAN WEYDEN:
I don't believe that that's your real reason.

358. CLOSE SHOT   LARSEN
as Larsen's face goes black with rage.

LARSEN:
I don't care what you believe...he stays on this ship.

There is a long pause.

VAN WEYDEN'S VOICE:
(o.s.)
He saw himself as a great figure...

LARSEN:
(bewildered)
What are you talking about?

359. MEDIUM CLOSE   VAN WEYDEN AND LARSEN

VAN WEYDEN:
(slowly)
I'm reading you the last part of my book.

There is another pause.

VAN WEYDEN:
(continuing)
"Better to reign in Hell than serve in Heaven"...

LARSEN:
(his face aglow with excitement)
Yeah...yeah...that's it...that's it. That's what it all adds up to..."Better to reign in Hell, than serve in Heaven."

VAN WEYDEN:
(his voice becomes more intense)
He saw himself to the last, proud, defiant, strong, shaking his fist at the heavens as the waters of the ocean swept over his head. He liked this kind of death. It was fitting that he should die this way...dragging his enemies down with him...turning defeat into victory...the true death of a superman...

There is a pause.

LARSEN:
That how it ends?

VAN WEYDEN:
No...that's not how it ends...There's one more paragraph...
(he pauses)
As I stood there watching him, I felt sorry for him.

LARSEN:
(snarling)
I don't need anyone feeling sorry for me.

VAN WEYDEN:
In a few minutes he would be alone, forced to face the truth by himself.

LARSEN:
I know what the truth is.

VAN WEYDEN:
(continuing)
Then he'd see himself as he really was...a pathetic, broken hulk of what was once a man...

LARSEN:
(viciously)
Shut up!

VAN WEYDEN:
He'd have to admit to himself that there was nothing heroic in his death...that it was small and petty and cheap....that the only motivation behind all of it was fear.

LARSEN:
Shut up, I say! Shut up!!

VAN WEYDEN:
(his words cut)
That he was *afraid* to go on living...For now there was no longer his great strength to sustain him. Now he was blind and helpless...now he had to go to other people and ask for help. I remembered how he had reacted when I once told him that he wouldn't dare to expose that ego of his in another world...Now I know that I was right.

LARSEN:
No...that's not true...that's not true. I don't want to hear anymore, do you hear me? I don't want to hear anymore...

VAN WEYDEN:
So this was the end of "Wolf" Larsen...a pitiful, dismal, pathetic finish.

LARSEN:
(shouting)
I told you I didn't want to hear any more. I told you...

In his blind rage, he lifts the gun, fires several shots pointblank at Van Weyden.

360. to 366. OMITTED[133]

367. CLOSE SHOT   VAN WEYDEN
As the bullets strike Van Weyden, his body twitches like a puppet in a marionette show. He is about to slump to the floor, but

he grabs on to the door knob for support. He stands there for a moment, then slumps to the floor, out of scene.

368. CLOSE SHOT   RUTH   INTERIOR CORRIDOR
as the echo of the two shots resounds throughout the corridor. For an instant she stands petrified, a look of horror on her face; then she begins to run in the direction of the shots.

369. CLOSE SHOT   LARSEN
as he stands there, the gun in his hand. The room is filled with the smoke of the shots.

370. REVERSE ANGLE   THE DOOR   FROM LARSEN'S ANGLE
We see it as Larsen does, hazy and in a mist. For an instant the smoke lifts, the doorway becomes clear. Then the entire scene becomes black. Larsen has gone totally blind.

371. CLOSE SHOT   LARSEN
as he passes his hand over his eyes. He shakes his head like a huge shaggy dog. Then he starts forward. CAMERA MOVES WITH him as he moves toward the door, gropingly, feeling for familiar objects in the room.

372. CLOSE SHOT   DOOR
as Larsen reaches it. His hands feel its familiar contours. He looks around him, as only a blind man can, all his senses alert. He shuffles his feet on the floor as though expecting to find Van Weyden's body there. The floor below him is empty. He bends down, slowly, carefully, and feels about the floor. Suddenly Van Weyden's voice is HEARD o.s.:

> **VAN WEYDEN'S VOICE:**
> So now you can't even see shadows!

Larsen straightens up quickly. A look of terror appears on his face.

373. CLOSE SHOT   VAN WEYDEN
He has made his way to the table. He stands leaning against it. His breath comes in short gasps, his teeth grit. The beads of per-

spiration on his brow indicate the supreme effort he is making in keeping on his feet.

> **LARSEN'S VOICE:**
> *(o.s.)*
> Van Weyden...where are you?
>
> **VAN WEYDEN:**
> Here...at the table...

374. CLOSE SHOT   LARSEN
as he stands at the door completely bewildered. Suddenly o.s. is HEARD the sound of Ruth's footsteps and her voice:

> **RUTH'S VOICE:**
> Mr. Van Weyden...Mr. Van Weyden!!

As she approaches, Larsen suddenly slams the door shut, locks it, and stands with his back toward it.

375. MEDIUM CLOSE   LARSEN AND VAN WEYDEN
as Larsen turns towards Van Weyden.

> **LARSEN:**
> *(bewilderment in his voice)*
> I couldn't have missed...I saw you.
> I fired right at you.
>
> **VAN WEYDEN:**
> *(he speaks with quite an effort throughout the following scene)*
> It's hard to kill the truth, Larsen, isn't it?
> *(he pauses—grits his teeth)*
> I could have escaped if I wanted to.
>
> **LARSEN:**
> *(bewildered)*
> If you wanted to?
>
> **VAN WEYDEN:**
> *(slowly)*
> Yes...after you fired and missed...I could have run out of the room.

LARSEN:
That's right...you could've.

VAN WEYDEN:
A little while ago you asked me what my price was...
(another pause)
I'll tell it to you...the key to that storeroom...Leach's life.

375a. CLOSE SHOT   RUTH
as she keeps pushing at the door.

RUTH:
(her voice small with fear)
Mr. Van Weyden! Mr. Van Weyden!
(her voice rises in intensity)
Mr. Van Weyden! Answer me!!

375b. MEDIUM CLOSE   INTERIOR   LARSEN'S CABIN   FAVORING LARSEN

VAN WEYDEN:
(shouting to Ruth)
It's all right, Ruth...everything's going to be all right. Stay at that door...don't go away.
(he turns back to Larsen)
Well...what do you say, Larsen?

LARSEN:
I don't know what you're getting at.

VAN WEYDEN:
(laughing)
It's simple. I want to prove to you how completely wrong you were, about everything...even about me. I'll strike a bargain with you. My life for Leach's.

There is a pause.

VAN WEYDEN:[134]
I stay here and die with you.

(he grips the table tighter)
Leach goes free.

LARSEN:
You're trying to trick me.

VAN WEYDEN:
The door is locked. You've still got two bullets left in that gun.

376. CLOSE SHOT LARSEN
Over his face comes a look of complete bewilderment. He hits his head with his fist as though trying to hammer the meaning of what has just happened into his brain.

LARSEN:
It's a trick. Nobody does anything like that for anybody unless they get something out of it.
(he is bewildered)
Maybe you think I'll unlock the door—let you go? Is that your idea? Maybe you think I'll give up my side of the bargain. Maybe you think I'll relent that you'll find some way—that you won't go down with me and the "Ghost"—I had it all figured out. I can't be wrong now—There must be a catch in it.

The boat lurches again as she settles lower into the water. O.S. comes Ruth's frantic banging on the door.

VAN WEYDEN:
There's no catch, Larsen. I'll go down with you and the "Ghost." Push the key through the door and see. Are you frightened I may prove you wrong?

377. CLOSE SHOT LARSEN
He looks like a man who just doesn't understand what is happening. His whole world in a few short seconds has crumbled. Almost mechanically he shrugs his shoulders, then takes out the key to the storeroom and, bending down, shoves it through the opening.

VAN WEYDEN'S VOICE:
(shouting)
Ruth! It's the key to the storeroom...did you get it?

378. MEDIUM CLOSE OFFICERS' MESS
as Ruth stoops down to get the key.

RUTH:
...Yes, I got it.

379. CLOSE SHOT INTERIOR LARSEN'S CABIN VAN WEYDEN
Van Weyden is using all his strength to keep on his feet.

VAN WEYDEN:
Go...quickly...get him out...quickly...before it's too late.

380. CLOSE SHOT RUTH AT DOOR
as she hesitates.

RUTH:
And you, Mr. Van Weyden?...What about you?

381. CLOSE SHOT VAN WEYDEN

VAN WEYDEN:
(slowly)
I'll meet you...
(he pauses)
On deck.

382.) CLOSE SHOT LARSEN

383.) as he stands still at the door, a bewildered, pathetic hulk of a man. His head keeps shaking from side to side as though he is trying to solve a riddle.

LARSEN:[135]
(softly)
Van Weyden?
(there is no answer)

Van Weyden?
(still no answer)
Van Weyden...where are you?
(the same quiet. His voice takes on a frenzied rhythm)
Van Weyden...where are you? Van Weyden...where are you?
(he almost shrieks the last word)
Van Weyden!!

384. WIDER ANGLE
as Larsen starts to move in the direction of Van Weyden. Suddenly he stops. Slowly he bends down. There on the floor is the dead body of Van Weyden, only silhouetted against the CAMERA.

385. CLOSE SHOT   LARSEN'S SHADOW ON THE WALL
as he bends down over the body of Van Weyden. We SEE his hand moving over his body . . . we see it withdrawn as it comes in contact with the blood that is still flowing from Van Weyden's wounds.

386. CLOSE SHOT   LARSEN
A mad look comes into his eyes.

LARSEN:
So it was a trick! I did hit you...I did hit you...I knew there was a catch in it...some place.
(his voice rises triumphantly. His fist is clenched in defiance)
I knew it!![136]

387. EXTERIOR DECK
as Ruth and Leach emerge from the hold. They stare around them wildly for an instant. (NOTE: This first part to be shot straight on Stage 21. Second half of scene with boat sinking— PROCESS-MINIATURE combination.)

        RUTH:
        Mr. Van Weyden! Where are you? Where are you?!

There is no answer. She turns to Leach. They both start going toward the stern of the boat. As they start forward, the boat lists again. The stern becomes almost completely submerged. They cling desperately to the railing.

        LEACH:
        (pointing off)
        It's no use! We're too late.[137]

388. CLOSE SHOT   THE STERN
It lies completely submerged under the water.

                                                        DISSOLVE TO:

389. INTERIOR DORY   SHOOTING TOWARDS THE "GHOST" (PROCESS)
as Leach and Ruth sit in the boat watching the "Ghost" slowly sink into the ocean. It seems to quiver for an instant, and hangs as though suspended in mid-air; then it is gone. As it disappears from view, the sun begins to break through the fog, revealing in the distance the island that Larsen spoke about— looking for all the world like a mirage, as we

                                                              FADE OUT.

THE END

Notes

Notes

The following notes delineate changes to the screenplay made during the production of the film.

1. Leach does not find shelter in the shadows of a tenement doorway. He is headed for the 8 Bells Bar when he stops and looks furtively over his shoulder at the camera.
2. When Leach enters the saloon a female singer, whom we never see, is heard singing "Hello, My Baby." Later in the scene she is heard singing "Rosie, You Are My Posie."
3. In the film Johnson's entire speech is omitted.
4. The following is cut out from Johnson's reply: "from what men say that is not possible aboard the "Ghost." (pride in his voice) I am an able seaman...I can still choose the kind of ship I sail on."
5. "Buddy" becomes "brother" in the film.
6. "I don't like to drink alone" is changed to "Oh, I just don't like to drink alone." This is a typical on-the-set change. Most such minor changes, unless they seem important, will be omitted from now on.
7. In the film Leach says "Yeah" and Svenson says "Come on down" instead of "hop in."
8. Svenson says "Yeah" instead of nodding. Here and above the small changes are essential because it's too dark and too foggy to see the nodding of heads.
9. What follows is changed to "tear out with your fingers the cold, merciless 'eart of Wolf Larsen."
10. The man does not take out a gun and level it at Leach, and the threat that follows is cut out.
11. In these scenes (25 to 33), omitted both from the final screenplay and the film, a stranger appears on deck and begins talking to Van Weyden. Angrily denouncing the pleasure craft in the fog-bound bay, he foreshadows the crashing of the ocean liner into the ferry. The man appears in the novel as well as earlier treatments.

12. "Yes?" becomes "Well?" in the film. This indicates a greater degree of irritation.
13. In the novel, the heroine's name is Maud Brewster; in the film it's Ruth Webster. In the novel the heroine is a lady; in the film she's an escaped convict. Was the original name deemed too refined for the tough broad Lupino plays? Are we to assume that she chooses to pass herself off as Maud because *she* thinks it is refined?
14. This line is cut from the film.
15. Ruth's speech is cut from the film.
16. In the film Van Weyden merely says "Don't!"
17. In Scene 55, omitted both from the final screenplay and the film, the stranger in note 11 appears again: "He, too, is caught in the vise of the crowd. He sees Van Weyden, shakes his head and solemnly raises his hand, as though bidding him hail and farewell. Then the crowd sweeps him from sight."
18. In the film Van Weyden merely says "Help! Ahoy! Ahoy!"
19. Scenes 62 through 67 are not in the film.
20. In the film this becomes "This man lying here…"
21. Scene 81 and most of Scene 82 are not in the film. Scene 82 begins with "Any of you fellows got a Bible or prayer book?"
22. In Scene 85, omitted both from the final screenplay and the film, there is a long shot of the ocean and "off the starboard side of the boat, not too far distant, a group of naked rocks thrusts above the sea. On top of them is a lighthouse. Not far from the lighthouse can be seen the sails of a schooner."
23. This is cut to "That's the pilot boat, isn't it?"
24. In the film, "You're that man," is added.
25. Cooky telling the captain that the "sack of coal'll be up in a minute" makes no sense now since the reference to "coal" and why it was needed was cut from the film.
26. In the film the preceding two lines are reversed.
27. In the film Van Weyden merely says, "Ahoy! Pilot boat! Ahoy!"

28. Scenes 95 through 98 are cut from the film, though we do catch a glimpse of Svenson sewing up the dead first mate in the canvas.

29. In the film this is changed to "If the descriptions fit you..."

30. In the film this exchange is as follows:
    VAN WEYDEN:
    Whether I've met her or not is none of your concern. Give me those notes!
    COOKY:
    I told you it's my duty to turn 'em over to the proper authorities.
    VAN WEYDEN:
    Give me those! You're not only a common thief, you're an informer as well.

31. Instead of slapping Van Weyden, Cooky kicks him in the stomach-lower chest area.

32. Cooky's dialogue here is cut from the film.

33. The ship's lamp does not swing violently, and we do not feel or see the "violent motion of the boat." Like most scenes in the film we have the feeling that the ship is in dry dock, motionless.

34. Since the boat is not pitching at all, Van Weyden has no difficulty in maintaining his balance. Nor does he spill the contents of a plate over Svenson. Van Weyden *is* shown serving the men, but the rest of scenes 108 and 109 are not in the film.

35. In the film Svenson says, "Ya told me to keep discipline aboard and I was afraid of trouble when we signed him up in 'Frisco. He was inciting a mutiny."

36. In the film Larsen doesn't mention the name of his brother's ship at this point.

37. In the film Larsen says "No, it's all right. He can wait. You don't have to do anything. It's all right."

38. In the film Louie says, "Oh my patient. She's improving. Her condition was rather serious."

39. In the film the room is dim but not "in complete darkness."

Van Weyden does not strike a match, he simply turns up the lamp, which is hanging from the ceiling.

40. To quicken the film's pace Warner Brothers even cut Milton:

> Here at least
> We shall be free, *th' Almighty hath not built*
> *Here for his envy, will not drive us hence*:
> Here we may reign secure, and in my choice
> To reign is worth ambition though in Hell:
> Better to reign in Hell, than serve in Heav'n.

The italicized text is cut both from the screenplay and from the film.

41. In the film this scene is changed somewhat:
    LARSEN:
    That's a great poem, isn't it?
    VAN WEYDEN:
    Yes, it's a great poem.
    LARSEN:
    Read me some of it.
    VAN WEYDEN:
    "Here at least we shall be free. Here we may reign secure and in my choice to reign is worth ambition though in Hell."
    LARSEN:
    "Better to reign in Hell than serve in Heaven."
    That's a great line. Milton really understood the devil. Sit down. This is the first time you've ever been in my cabin, isn't it?
    Then the scene continues as in the screenplay.

42. Larsen adds "How much?" here.

43. The whistling and "That's quite a lot" are not in the film.

44. In the film this line is changed to "Yes, but you wouldn't have to earn all that money."

45. There is no knock on the door and Larsen says nothing. Leach simply opens the door and gives his message.

46. At this point it looks like someone merely tosses a bucket of

water through the porthole. The lights aren't extinguished and for "An 'eavy sea" no more water comes through the porthole throughout the scene and we barely detect any movement of the ship.

47. Larsen's "Keep awake...you drunken..." followed by Louie's "Don't hit me...don't hit me" are not in the film.

48. There are both cuts and changes in this scene:
    VAN WEYDEN:
    (gently) I'll say it.
    RUTH:
    Don't let them take me back. Don't let them take me back. You don't know what it's like being in prison. I'd rather die. I'd rather die first.
    It's at this point that Ruth lapses into unconsciousness again (Scene 135) and Cooky says "Strike me pink! A convict," etc.

49. In the film Larsen's speech ends here.

50. "A horrible dream" becomes "the horrible dream."

51. This sentence is omitted from the film.

52. "Forlorn" is omitted—a good example of stripping the film of all excess verbiage.

53. Instead of this Louie says, "No, no. I can't. My hands. I need..."

54. Larsen's cynical remark is not in the film.

55. "Alike" becomes "the same."

56. "Funny, ain't it?" is not in the film.

57. A blood transfusion at sea, and without the proper equipment, is both ludicrous and anachronistic. The film takes place in 1900 when even laboratory transfusions were rare experiments.

58. All the scenes dealing with the young boy are omitted. In the previous screenplay (the omitted scenes 149, 150, 151) Larsen commands the boy to "Get up to the mast and clear that rigging!" The boy begins to climb up the mast, gets dizzy, and is pulled back down by Leach. Leach offers to do the work for him. Oddly enough, in the novel Leach is the "boy" who is ordered to climb up the mast. We never see the boy in the film. The film jumps to Scene 155, with Cooky's "hysterical cackling."

59. This speech of Louie's is cut from the film.

60. The dialogue here is changed a bit until Ruth says "I'm very grateful, young man." It follows:
    RUTH:
    I'd like to thank the sailor who gave his blood.
    LOUIE:
    Yes, yes. Young man!
    LEACH:
    The name is Leach.
    LOUIE:
    Excuse me...my memory. Here he is.

61. This sentence is cut from the film.

62. This sentence is changed to "Certainly."

63. At this point in the film Cooky replies "Aye, sir."

64. Here and below, Ruth's dialogue in the film is changed to "No, wait a minute, wait a minute. Gimme a break, will ya? Will ya?" The rest of the scene is cut and is picked up again when Leach throws the marlin spike at Larsen.

65. In the film Van Weyden does not shout out a warning.

66. All the following is cut from the film until Scene 179, in the captain's cabin, when Van Weyden begins to speak.

67. The omitted scene, which appears in the previous draft but not the film, is as follows:
    WIDER ANGLE as he (Larsen) paces the room.
    LARSEN:
    (accusingly) You're an onlooker of life...you've never taken part in it...all the ideas you have about it are false...(suddenly) I claim there's no such thing as truth and justice and respect and dignity...they're words without meaning. I claim there's only the desire...the will to live. That's the thing that drives man on...and for that he'll do anything...pay any price... just to live...to exist...to crawl...(he turns to Van Weyden, facing him across the table). That woman...she talks about going to another country to start a new life...she knows in her heart and soul that the new life won't be any different than the old...that she'll walk

the streets of Shanghai like she walked the streets of 'Frisco. And people will degrade her and spit at her. But she won't kill herself...she'll go on living...until she decays.

In Scene 179, which immediately follows what Larsen says above, a portion of Van Weyden's dialogue is also omitted from the final screenplay and from the film:

> **VAN WEYDEN:**
> *(slowly)* You're right, sir. I am an onlooker...a sort of detached, isolated person. I stand off from life and form my little theories about it. They have no passion in them...their only virtue is that they're purely objective.

Larsen's speech, while too long, at least according to Warner Brothers' standards for an "action" film, helps us to understand Van Weyden's remark immediately after Louie commits suicide and also clarifies the final confrontation between Larsen and Van Weyden.

68. Here Larsen says "What!"

69. "Board" becomes "deck" in the film.

70. This is not in the film.

71. This is not in the film.

72. This line is changed to "All right, Louie, I'll talk to the men."

73. "Captain" is substituted for "Wolf." Louie wouldn't dare call Larsen "Wolf."

74. In the film this scene, until Larsen kicks Louie, is changed somewhat:

    > **LARSEN:**
    > Now, listen everybody. Louie's come to me with a complaint. He's not being treated the way he thinks he should be. I don't want you laughing at him or at his clothes.
    > **LOUIE:**
    > Tell them about calling me Louie.
    > **LARSEN:**
    > Oh, yes. He's not to be called Louie anymore. From now on it's doctor. (Turning to Louie) Doctor what?

> LOUIE:
> Doctor Prescott. Doctor Louis J. Prescott.
> LARSEN:
> Oh. Doctor Prescott. He's to be given all the courtesy and respect due a physician of his standing. That satisfactory, Doctor Prescott?
> LOUIE:
> Quite satisfactory, Captain Larsen. Thank you very much.
> LARSEN:
> Yeh.

75. The last two sentences are not in the film.

76. In Louie's speech "You below there" and "I'll come down the way I want to" are not in the film.

77. In this scene there are quite a few changes.

> LOUIE:
> You'll regret the day you ever tried to make a fool of Louie. Hey, ask him why it is this ship doesn't sail the regular ship lanes, why she scurries like a rat at the sight of another boat.
> LARSEN:
> Come down!
> LOUIE:
> When I'm good and ready. You won't answer any of these questions, will you, Larsen. But I will! There'll be less of you come back from this voyage than went on it. I can promise you that. Hey Larsen. Tell 'em about your brother, Death Larsen. Tell 'em about the fear that comes into your heart at the mention of his name.
> LARSEN:
> I fear no man, no man!
> LOUIE:
> Tell 'em about the oath he's taken to kill you. Tell 'em about his ship, the "Macedonia." Tell 'em about the cannon he's got on board it, primed to blow you, your boat and all on board to kingdom come.
> LARSEN:
> Louie, come down.

LOUIE:
I'll come down, in my own way. Hey, look!
At this point the film jumps to Scene 202, where Louie hurls himself to the deck.

78. This is changed to "I thought you might like a cigarette."

79. This is cut from the film.

80. This is changed to "Look, why don't you try and get some rest."

81. "That drink" is cut out. So is Scene 203f because she hasn't brought him anything to drink. Also, Leach's "the cigarettes" is cut out.

82. This is changed to "Hold it, will ya?"

83. The scene changes quite a bit here. Ruth doesn't begin to cry and Leach continues talking: "You don't have to go back to the States. There's an iron gate waiting there to shut me in too." Then Ruth concludes the scene with "Oh." (She sighs) "Inside or out it's all the same. To be free...to be let alone...to live in peace, even if only for a little while. Like this. But I don't expect that anymore." Ruth does quite a bit of weeping in the screenplay, but not in the film. Lupino makes her tougher.

84. Scenes 204 through 207 are omitted. The action picks up again with Scene 207b.

85. This is omitted here but appears below. Also, Svenson doesn't take Larsen by surprise. Larsen calls out "Svenson" and then continues with the line in note 87 below.

86. This is omitted but appears below (see note 88).

87. This is changed to "Johnson said you wanted to see me."

88. Here Svenson now adds, "Your attacks are getting worse, ain't they, sir?" Larsen replies, "I didn't ask for your opinion."

89. We don't hear any sobbing and Cooky says nothing and does not hurl a shoe against the wall.

90. It's during this scene that Ruth is wearing either a nightgown or a camisole. When she was rescued she could have been wearing a camisole beneath her jacket, blouse, or skirt, but not a nightgown. Later we see her wearing a turtleneck sweater. But

it looks old and ragged and masculine and Leach might have given it to her.

91. The first part of Leach's reply is cut and picks up at this point.
92. Though Larsen returns from the sea, Svenson does not. Leach was one of the men involved in dumping him overboard. Yet at the end he goes scot-free! The censors must have been napping because in 1941 a murderer was supposed to pay for his crime with his life.
93. This line is not in the film.
94. The first part of this sentence is cut and a "sir" is added.
95. In the film this is "I wouldn't make a good mate, sir."
96. This, and Johnson's reply, are not in the film.
97. This line is cut. It makes Larsen look like a coward and Larsen would never admit to being a coward.
98. The entire scene with the boy is not in the film.
99. In scenes 228, 229 and 230 we hear no dialogue distinctly. All we hear are muffled words, grunts, groans, and the sounds of a struggle.
100. This scene is filmed as follows:
    LEACH:
    Stop bellyachin'. You shoulda thought of that before you joined us.
    HARRISON:
    Well, I didn't. I'm thinkin' of it now. I'll tell him who put us up to it. I'll tell him.
    LEACH:
    You don't have to tell him. I'll tell him myself. And if I have to, I'll go out like Louie, thumbin' my nose at him. You've all forgotten about Louie, haven't you? You're all too busy worryin' about what's gonna happen to you. Well, nothin's gonna happen to you. He needs you to sail his ship for him. He needs you to break your backs for him. Maybe someday you'll get wise to that.
    MATE'S VOICE:
    Van Weyden! Are you down there?

Then we continue with Scene 233 when Harrison says, "No, he isn't." In the film Harrison speaks in place of the sailor.

101. Scenes 234 through 237 are not in the film. The scene begins with Larsen saying, "Cooky, I want the names of all the men who were in on this."

102. Larsen's speech is changed to the following: "Do it now, Van Weyden. Go ahead, stick the knife into him. Is this the first time you ever wanted to commit murder? Good feeling, isn't it, huh? To know that you hold a man's life in your hands. You enjoyed it. Didn't you?" Then the scene continues with Van Weyden saying, "I think I know now why men call you 'Wolf.' "

103. Larsen's line is omitted.

104. Van Weyden's line is omitted.

105. "I want to know you're still here" is changed to "That's it."

106. "After my death" is changed to "after you got rid of me."

107. This sentence is omitted.

108. Scenes 253 through 257 are compressed and are changed considerably:

    LARSEN:
    I know exactly how you felt. What Louie told you the other day was absolutely true. Every word of it. I have no intentions of hunting any seals. I leave that to my brother. Sure my brother has cannon on board. Sure he's got 'em primed to sink the "Ghost." Sure there's a chance of all of you going down with the ship. But also, there's just as good a chance that you won't. And that means we get a cargo of seal skins the likes of which you've never seen before. You see, that's the joke. We steal them from the same people who buy them. Certainly you have no scruples against stealing if you get your share of the loot. If this voyage turns out well, you'll each have enough to keep you for the rest of your lives. I promise you that. Van Weyden, we'll open up the liquor stores for the men. Give them all they want. Oh yes, there's one more thing I feel I ought to warn you about. You have an informer in your midst. There's nothing I detest more than an in-

Notes to Pages 126–143

former. As evidence of my good faith I'm going to tell you who he is. Cooky gave me this list.
COOKY:
(screaming) Ye dirty...ye black 'earted devil!
CREWMAN:
Get that squealer!

109. Nobody says these things. There's merely a jumble of noise.

110. Here we have no account of what happens in omitted scenes 269, 270, and 271. In the previous screenplay Larsen is near Cooky, looking down at him. Then "Cooky, with a scream of rage like a wounded animal, flounders a few feet over to Larsen's legs and buries his teeth in Larsen's leg." This scene also appears in the original novel. In the film, scenes 272 through 276 are also omitted.

111. Instead of this Leach says, "One sound and you're a dead man."

112. "The one hanging over that bunk" is omitted.

113. Instead of this Johnson merely says, "Leave him alone." Van Weyden and Leach are actually in silhouette. We cannot really see Van Weyden's reactions in the film.

114. Van Weyden doesn't say "you fools."

115. This last sentence is omitted.

116. Here Leach says, "Johnson, get this stuff in the boat." Then to Van Weyden he says, "Do you still want to go with us?" Van Weyden says "Yes" and Leach closes the scene with "I'll go get Ruth."

117. It's during this escape scene that, for the first and only time, the sea is rough. But the water spraying the players seems to be coming from a hose, not from the sea; and even in this scene the ship rocks hardly at all.

118. This exchange between Smoke and Larsen is cut and begins again with Smoke saying, "They'll soon catch up to us."

119. Larsen is not at the wheel here and he does not tell Smoke to take the wheel. We do not see who is at the wheel, but Larsen

yells to whoever it is to "Make for the fog bank off the starboard bow! Head straight into her!"

120. Scenes from this point through 297s are omitted. In the film Cooky trips up Larsen by using his crutch. Larsen does fall to the deck but immediately recovers his balance.

121. Scenes 298 through 319 are omitted.

122. These scenes are omitted from the final screenplay and from the film. They merely show the horizon becoming lighter and lighter and Van Weyden "desperately trying to fight off going to sleep" while Johnson, at the helm, smiles at him. Van Weyden smiles faintly back and then looks off in the direction of the prow. Then the "camera holds on him as bit by bit his head drops to his chest."

123. This is cut from the film. Scenes 338 to 342 are also abbreviated. Leach does not carry a knife. He explores the deck of the "Ghost" warily and also sees the body of a sailor hidden beneath a fallen mast.

124. At this point Larsen slams and locks the door behind Leach and Leach yells out, "Open that door!"

125. Scene 345 is cut until the point where Ruth shouts, "George! George!!"

126. What Ruth and Van Weyden say in the following three exchanges is omitted. The scene picks up again with Van Weyden saying, "Stay here."

127. Ruth's lines two and three are omitted.

128. "That should prove to you I can still see" is added here.

129. This second question is omitted.

130. "I can understand your actions" is added here.

131. The dialogue from here until Van Weyden says, "Leach...what about Leach?" is omitted.

132. The dialogue from here until Van Weyden says, "He saw himself as a great figure" is omitted.

133. The omitted screenplay scenes, also absent from the film, are as follows:

RUTH:
(frantically) Mr. Van Weyden...I've found him! I've found him! Mr. Van Weyden, where are you?
VAN WEYDEN:
(from Larsen's cabin) Keep out of sight of the door... he's got a gun!
RUTH:
(her voice filled with terror) Larsen?
VAN WEYDEN'S VOICE:
Yes.
RUTH:
He's locked in the hold. I've got to get him out. The water's coming up too fast. He'll drown...I've got to get him out. I tried to break the door down...It was too heavy.
LARSEN:
(smiling) There's good strong doors aboard my ship.
RUTH:
The key...I've got to have the key.
LARSEN:
I've got the key...here...Come and take it from me, Mr. Van Weyden.
RUTH'S VOICE:
I'll take it from him...gun or no gun.
VAN WEYDEN:
Ruth! Don't come in here! *(he turns to Larsen)* Larsen...you don't have to go down with this ship. You can still save yourself. We'll take care of you ...we'll take you ashore. I give you my word.
LARSEN:
No...I stay here. I'm not going to live out the rest of my days...a blind man...a beggar...nobody's going to pity me...I've lived like I want to. I'll die like I want to.
VAN WEYDEN:
All right then...die alone! Why take others with you?
LARSEN:
Why?...Why? I don't know...It isn't something I thought about. Up to the time you came back on board this vessel, I was perfectly willing to die alone.

> Then as soon as I heard Leach sneaking aboard, I knew...I knew that that was the way for me to die...pulling everything down with me...this vessel... you...Leach...the girl...You explain that, Mr. Writer... you're so good at explaining things...(Suddenly the boat lists sharply. Larsen holds on to the table for support. Van Weyden is thrown to the floor.) She's sinking fast, Mr. Van Weyden.
> **VAN WEYDEN:**
> *(as he regains his feet)* Ruth...get on that boat. I'll get the key. I'll get Leach out...wait for us...save yourself.
> **RUTH:**
> Save myself? For what? He's the beginning and the end of the only part of my life that's ever meant anything to me. If he lives...I live. If he dies...I die. That's the way it is with me. Maybe you're afraid of that gun...I'm not.

This section is too talky and too melodramatic. The decision to cut it was a wise one.

134. The dialogue from here until Larsen says, "I had it all figured out," is omitted.

135. This scene isn't played as hysterically and as melodramatically as it sounds and three of the "Van Weydens" have been cut. Furthermore, Van Weyden does fall to the floor when Larsen shoots him. But he rises to his feet and seats himself as he speaks to Larsen in his dying moments. After Larsen calls to him, Van Weyden falls to the floor.

136. At this point Larsen is standing, waiting to meet death, as water bursts into the cabin and the walls cave in around him. He meets death unflinchingly and is made to seem almost heroic.

137. At this point Ruth says, "Oh, no!"

In 1936 after theatrical experience on Broadway, Robert Rossen (1908–1966) became a screenwriter for Warner Brothers. Prior to his first directing assignment *Johnny O'Clock* (1947), he wrote scripts for many Warner Brothers social consciousness movies such as *Marked Woman, They Won't Forget* (both 1937), *Dust Be My Destiny, The Roaring Twenties* (both 1939), and *Out of the Fog* (1941). Rossen also wrote screenplays for *A Walk in the Sun, The Strange Love of Martha Ivers* (both 1946) and later directed *Body and Soul* (1947) and *All the King's Men* (1949). He coscripted *The Treasure of Sierra Madre* (1948) but received no screen credit. After testifying before the House Committee on Un-American Activities, he went on to direct three critically disappointing films: *Alexander the Great* (1956), *Island in the Sun* (1957), and *They Came to Cordura* (1959). Rossen later moved towards depictions of the human personality, receiving critical acclaim for his last two films, *The Hustler* and *Lilith* (both 1964).

Rocco Fumento is a professor emeritus of English, creative writing, and film studies at the University of Illinois at Urbana. Aside from publishing many short stories and film articles, he has published two novels and a book on creative writing and has edited the Warner Brothers screenplay for *42nd Street*.

Tony Williams is an associate professor and the area head of film studies in the Department of English, Southern Illinois University at Carbondale. Author of *Jack London: The Movies* (1992), *Hearths of Darkness: The Family in the American Horror Film* (1996), and *Larry Cohen: Radical Allegories of an American Filmmaker* (1997), he has written several articles on film and contributed to the *Jack London Newsletter* and *The Jack London Journal*. He was the Popular Culture Association area head of *Jack London's Life and Works* (1989–1994) and is currently editing Jack London's unfinished novel *Cherry*.